What Jesus Taught About Manifesting Abundance

**". . . wisdom, but not the kind
that comes from here on earth. . ."**
1 Corinthians 2:6, TLB

by
John Avanzini

Harrison House
Tulsa, Oklahoma

What Jesus Taught About Manifesting Abundance
ISBN: 0-89274-941-5
First Printing: 250,000

Unless otherwise indicated, all Scripture quotations are
taken from the *King James Version* of the Bible.

Verses marked TLB are taken from *The Living Bible*.
Copyright © 1971. Used by permission of Tyndale House
Publishers, Inc., Wheaton, Illinois 60189. All rights
reserved.

Verses marked **Amplified** are Scripture taken from THE
AMPLIFIED BIBLE, Old Testament copyright © 1965,
1987 by The Zondervan Corporation. The Amplified New
Testament copyright © 1958, 1987 by The Lockman
Foundation. Used by permission.

For emphasis, the author has placed selected words from
the Bible quotations in italics.

Harrison House
P.O. Box 35035
Tulsa, OK 74153

I respectfully dedicate this book to
Kenneth and Gloria Copeland.

Contents

Foreword

It's one thing to *talk about* having our needs met, and quite another to *actually have them met!* How many times have we been blessed with a soul-stirring message on abundance, only to realize that we *still* have many unmet needs?

Enter John Avanzini's latest book, *What Jesus Taught About Manifesting Abundance.* You have asked, "How do I actually get the promised abundance of God in my hand?" Good question, and that is really what this book is all about.

One of the most shocking revelations is the fact that God is not moved by my need—as urgent or as great as that need may be! *What?* Isn't He ". . . **touched with the feeling of our infirmities**" (Hebrews 4:15)? Yes, Jesus often touches and heals because of His love and compassion for suffering humanity—thank God! He was also moved with compassion for the multitudes, because they were **"scattered abroad, as sheep having no shepherd"** (Matthew 9:36).

But when it comes to actually manifesting material abundance in our lives, God is moved only by our faith and our action.

Give, and it shall be given unto you. . . .
Luke 6:38

Oh, how the heresy hunters rant and rage against this truth. But as I have said so often, anytime a truth is violently attacked by the "pharisees" of today, we had better take another look. Satan does not bother to attack anything that has no truth and that will not harm his kingdom!

In *What Jesus Taught About Manifesting Abundance,* the simple truth of *how* we get the provision and abundance of God in our possession is clearly and scripturally laid out, step by step, as only John Avanzini can do it. Please read and study this message carefully and prayerfully so that you can have *all* your needs met. Not only that, but God's superabundance will be yours so that you will also have **". . . plenty left over to give joyfully to others"** (2 Corinthians 9:8, TLB).

Paul F. Crouch, President
Trinity Broadcasting Network

1

Too Good to Be True

. . . they were all amazed at the mighty
power of God. . . .

Luke 9:43

Imagine getting back thirty dollars for giving a dollar,
six thousand dollars for giving a hundred, a hundred
thousand dollars or more for giving a thousand. This rate of
return sounds impossible to most folks. Does it sound
impossible to you? Well, it didn't seem the least bit
impossible to Jesus. In fact, He actually taught these
outrageous rates of increase.

I want to begin our time together in this book by
making a special promise to you. If you will read this
material with an open mind and faithfully put its principles
to work, you will be able to manifest these same increases
in your own finances.

Powerful Revelation

The information I will be sharing with you is a
powerful revelation. Please note I am not using the word
revelation loosely. I use it in its strongest sense. What you
are about to read is a body of truth I received directly from
our Lord. Now mind you, it's not a new truth, it's neglected
truth.

It is also a breakthrough truth! I say it is for two
reasons. First, I say it is because of the person who speaks

it. He is Jesus Christ Himself. Secondly, I say it is because of the tremendous detail He goes into when teaching it.

Two Key Verses

The great truth I am speaking of comes from the fourth chapter of Mark. This chapter contains two key verses that should have immediately put us on notice as to their extreme importance. Even though these verses have been crying out to the Church for two thousand years, no one seems to have paid any attention to them.

After all these years of study, I can't recall a single teaching about them. Let me be quick to take my part of the blame. In thirty years of ministry, I never placed any special emphasis on them either, that is, until now.

When you fully realize the magnitude of these verses, you cannot help but wonder why you haven't heard more about them.

The Doctrine of Jesus

We find the first of these wondrous sayings in verse 2.

And he taught them many things by parables, and said unto them in *his doctrine*.
Mark 4:2

Think of what you just read. Verse 2 says Jesus is about to reveal His doctrine to us!

I am convinced the main reason we have gone this long without emphasizing the significance of this statement is that it deals with *doctrine*. So much division has taken place over doctrine that most Christians subconsciously tend to avoid it.

The Importance of Doctrine

Please hear me carefully. I am not minimizing the importance of Bible doctrines. It is impossible to study the Word of God without realizing they exist. The problem is that men have clouded the simple truth of God's Word by coming up with so many opposing doctrines.

Catholics have developed doctrines, and Baptists have done the same. Methodists have them, as well as Lutherans. The denominations all have their own distinctive doctrines, each one being different from the others.

What Doctrine Is

Let's take a moment and define what a doctrine is. Simply stated, it is what an individual or group of individuals understand about the Scripture. To know what Presbyterians understand about God's Word, you must study Presbyterian doctrine. To know what Episcopalians believe, you must study Episcopalian doctrine, and so forth throughout the denominations.

What Jesus Understood

With this definition of *doctrine,* let me once again draw your attention to verse 2.

And he taught them many things by parables, and said unto them in *his doctrine.*
Mark 4:2

This portion of Scripture is of tremendous importance because it alerts us that Jesus will be telling us about His doctrine. If I know anything about Bible study, I know its primary purpose is to promote understanding of what Jesus (God) is teaching. We want to understand the mind of Christ.

> **Let this mind be in you, which was also in**
> **Christ Jesus.**
> **Philippians 2:5**

Well, there it is in black and white. Mark 4:2 says Jesus is about to reveal some of the things He understands.

The Key Parable

A second verse in this chapter should also have caught our attention. It deals with *parables.*

> **And he said unto them, Know ye not this**
> **parable? and *how then will ye know all parables?***
> **Mark 4:13**

Just think about it. Here we have the key that qualifies us to understand all parables. How is it that a verse with such tremendous promise could go virtually unnoticed for so long?

When I fully realized what these verses (2 and 13) were saying, I immediately began to study carefully the fourth chapter of Mark. I read it and reread it until I had all but memorized it. I also read everything written about it that I could find.

Broken, Disjointed Thoughts

The longer I studied it, the more confusing it became. I just kept coming up with the same conclusions. The chapter appeared to be made up of broken portions of unrelated information.

Now don't misunderstand. I saw powerful streams of truth in it. However, each time a flow of truth began, it seemed to stop abruptly.

Seeds, Bushels, Beds, and a Storm

I found the parable of the sower. Jesus told it and retold it. Then there was a verse about a candle, a bushel, and a bed. This verse alerted me to the fact that I should be careful about what I heard. The parable also gave me some information about the growth stages of an agricultural crop and the need for its timely harvest. It told me that a mustard seed could potentially grow into a very large tree. It could grow so big that birds could rest in its branches. The chapter ended with the story about a storm at sea and how Jesus stopped it.

After reading Mark 4 again and again, all I could see was a mixture of unrelated thoughts. I was not able to make the chapter even vaguely resemble the doctrine of Jesus, nor did I find in it the key to all the other parables.

Clear Vision on a Stormy Day

No matter how disjointed the chapter seemed, I kept on studying. My spirit kept telling me it contained something really big. This situation continued unchanged, until I heard Kenneth Copeland make a statement about Mark 4. I will always remember the circumstances of the day I heard him speak those key words.

It was the worst day in the winter of 1991. The roads in the Fort Worth area were covered in sheets of ice. Kenneth and Gloria were hosting their annual ministers' conference. The weather was so bad, it was a wonder anyone was able to make the journey out to their headquarters at Eagle Mountain. All the freeways were clogged. There were accidents everywhere. To be honest, I wanted to stay home. However, something inside compelled me to go.

I remember winding my way up and down back roads, trying to find a way that wasn't blocked by automobile accidents. When I finally arrived, the meeting had started, and Brother Copeland was teaching. In the midst of his discourse, he asked us to turn to Mark 4:21. He spoke no more than a dozen words, and the answers I needed came flooding into my spirit.

With all due respect to Brother Copeland, I didn't hear anything else he said from that point. With just a few choice words Brother Copeland had said, the Holy Spirit put the key I had been waiting for into my hand. It opened up the whole chapter to me. Months of study suddenly came into focus. Not only that, but the book you now hold in your hand was born.

In closing this chapter, let me say that the fourth chapter of Mark is most surely the doctrine of Jesus Christ. In it He keeps His promise to open the parables to us. The best part is that He shows us how to manifest abundance according to the principles of biblical economics.

2

The Overview

This portion of the book is a new experience for me, for I have never written anything like it before. In it I must somehow give you a brief overview of the forty-one verses that make up Mark 4. I must write this overview without quenching your appetite for the revelation that will follow.

Let's quickly review the chapter.

Mark 4

Verse 1:

> And he began again to teach by the sea side: and there was gathered unto him a great multitude, so that he entered into a ship, and sat in the sea; and the whole multitude was by the sea on the land.

When Mark opens the chapter, Jesus is speaking to a multitude at the seaside.

Verse 2:

> And he taught them many things by parables, and said unto them in his doctrine.

I have already alerted you to the major significance of this verse. The important thing here is that Jesus is about to give us His doctrine. He will be revealing a part of the mind of Christ.

Verses 3-8:

> **Hearken; Behold, there went out a sower to sow:**
>
> **And it came to pass, as he sowed, some fell by the way side, and the fowls of the air came and devoured it up.**
>
> **And some fell on stony ground, where it had not much earth; and immediately it sprang up, because it had no depth of earth:**
>
> **But when the sun was up, it was scorched; and because it had no root, it withered away.**
>
> **And some fell among thorns, and the thorns grew up, and choked it, and it yielded no fruit.**
>
> **And other fell on good ground, and did yield fruit that sprang up and increased; and brought forth, some thirty, and some sixty, and some an hundred.**

The parable of the sower is probably our Lord's best known discourse. He tells of four situations in which the sower places his seed. Three of these produce little or no harvest. However, one brings forth thirty, sixty, and even a hundredfold.

Verse 9:

> **And he said unto them, He that hath ears to hear, let him hear.**

Jesus closes this portion of the teaching by instructing the hearers to hear what He says. It is obvious from the context that He wants them to do more than just hear the sound of His voice. He wants them to understand fully what He is saying.

Verses 10-12:

> **And when he was alone, they that were about him with the twelve asked of him the parable.**
> **And he said unto them, Unto you it is given to know the mystery of the kingdom of God: but unto them that are without, all these things are done in parables:**
> **That seeing they may see, and not perceive; and hearing they may hear, and not understand; lest at any time they should be converted, and their sins should be forgiven them.**

Here Jesus identifies the ones who will be able to bring forth abundance. It will be those who understand.

Verse 13:

> **And he said unto them, Know ye not this parable? and how then will ye know all parables?**

Here He reveals the key to all the parables, for He says those who understand this one will be able to understand all of them.

Verses 14-20:

> **The sower soweth the word.**
> **And these are they by the way side, where the word is sown; but when they have heard, Satan cometh immediately, and taketh away the word that was sown in their hearts.**

> **And these are they likewise which are sown
> on stony ground; who, when they have heard the
> word, immediately receive it with gladness;**
>
> **And have no root in themselves, and so
> endure but for a time: afterward, when affliction
> or persecution ariseth for the word's sake,
> immediately they are offended.**
>
> **And these are they which are sown among
> thorns; such as hear the word,**
>
> **And the cares of this world, and the
> deceitfulness of riches, and the lusts of other
> things entering in, choke the word, and it
> becometh unfruitful.**
>
> **And these are they which are sown on good
> ground; such as hear the word, and receive it,
> and bring forth fruit, some thirtyfold, some
> sixty, and some an hundred.**

Notice when He repeats the parable, Jesus makes a small but significant change. The seed He now speaks of is no longer an agricultural seed. It is *the Word of God.* Notice carefully that the Word-seed responds in exactly the same way the agricultural seed does.

The notable truth here is that God gives the power to reproduce to whatever He calls a seed.

Verse 21:

> **And he said unto them, Is a candle brought
> to be put under a bushel, or under a bed? and
> not to be set on a candlestick?**

This verse is the one that tends to block the flow of the whole chapter. Traditional explanations do little to help, as the subject abruptly changes from sowing and reaping to beds, bushels, and candles. When you see what Jesus is actually saying in this verse, the roadblock immediately comes down, and all forty-one verses flow into one uninterrupted revelation.

Verse 22:

> **For there is nothing hid, which shall not be manifested; neither was any thing kept secret, but that it should come abroad.**

God wants to talk to you about the secrets of manifesting abundance.

Verse 23:

> **If any man have ears to hear, let him hear.**

Pay attention, for you will not understand the next two verses until you fully understand this one.

Verses 24,25:

> **And he said unto them, Take heed what ye hear: with what measure ye mete, it shall be measured to you: and unto you that hear shall more be given.**
> **For he that hath, to him shall be given: and he that hath not, from him shall be taken even that which he hath.**

When you understand the implied subject, a primary principle of biblical economics becomes yours.

Verses 26-29:

> **And he said, So is the kingdom of God, as if a man should cast seed into the ground;**

> And should sleep, and rise night and day, and the seed should spring and grow up, he knoweth not how.
>
> For the earth bringeth forth fruit of herself; first the blade, then the ear, after that the full corn in the ear.
>
> But when the fruit is brought forth, immediately he putteth in the sickle, because the harvest is come.

Understanding timing and seasons is necessary to manifest abundance.

Verses 30-34:

> And he said, Whereunto shall we liken the kingdom of God? or with what comparison shall we compare it?
>
> It is like a grain of mustard seed, which, when it is sown in the earth, is less than all the seeds that be in the earth:
>
> But when it is sown, it groweth up, and becometh greater than all herbs, and shooteth out great branches; so that the fowls of the air may lodge under the shadow of it.
>
> And with many such parables spake he the word unto them, as they were able to hear it.
>
> But without a parable spake he not unto them: and when they were alone, he expounded all things to his disciples.

The manifestation of abundance comes only to those who strictly obey God's Kingdom principles in the distribution of their harvest.

Verses 35-39:

> And the same day, when the even was come, he saith unto them, Let us pass over unto the other side.
>
> And when they had sent away the multitude, they took him even as he was in the ship. And there were also with him other little ships.
>
> And there arose a great storm of wind, and the waves beat into the ship, so that it was now full.
>
> And he was in the hinder part of the ship, asleep on a pillow: and they awake him, and say unto him, Master, carest thou not that we perish?
>
> And he arose, and rebuked the wind, and said unto the sea, Peace, be still. And the wind ceased, and there was a great calm.

The Apostle Mark now does the teaching. He points out the essential part a competent pastor plays in the manifestation of abundance.

Verses 40,41:

> And he said unto them, Why are ye so fearful? how is it that ye have no faith?
>
> And they feared exceedingly, and said one to another, What manner of man is this, that even the wind and the sea obey him?

The true pastor is not afraid to minister to the real problems of his sheep. He also never abandons the message of faith.

A Sketchy Overview

I realize this overview has been sketchy to say the least. However, I do hope it has shown you that these forty-one verses hold a greater truth than the mixed teaching of the traditional commentators. These verses contain one, continual, unbroken teaching that instructs the believer in our Lord's doctrine of manifesting abundance.

Let's now proceed with an expanded teaching of these marvelous verses.

3

The Sower

Sowing usually refers to planting agricultural seed. People throughout the world know the parable of the farmer who sowed his seed.

Four Possibilities

Jesus gives us four circumstances that might take place when the farmer plants agricultural seed. First, the seed can fall by the wayside and become food for the birds (verse 4). These seeds bring no harvest for man.

Next, Jesus tells of seed that falls into stony ground. It brings forth a sprout. However, the shallow ground is unable to sustain normal growth. Where there is no depth of soil, a proper root system cannot develop. This lack of soil causes the plant to wither long before it can bring forth any kind of fruit (verses 5 and 6).

Then Jesus tells about seed the farmer sows among thorns (verse 7). How foolish it seems to sow seed in a thorn patch. However, if you compare this account with the one in the Book of Luke, you see that thorn-infested soil can sometimes appear to be good ground. In Luke 8:7, the writer tells us the ground already contained the seed of weeds. Upon close observation, you will find that weeds don't actually appear until a crop begins to grow.

> . . . and the thorns *sprang up with it* [the
> seed], and choked it.
>
> **Luke 8:7**

After three failed attempts, the sower finally gets it
right. He sows into good ground and receives the miracle of
harvest-proportion returns.

> . . . other fell on good ground . . . and
> brought forth, some thirty, and some sixty, and
> some an hundred.
>
> **Mark 4:8**

Questions Arise

After He gave this purely agricultural illustration,
Jesus' disciples pondered the meaning of the story. Verse
10 tells us that as soon as they were alone, they asked the
Lord to explain the parable.

> . . . when he was alone, they that were about
> him . . . asked of him the parable.
>
> **Mark 4:10**

Knowing our Lord as they did, they were sure the
parable contained more than just agricultural information.

At this point Jesus relates to them the importance of
spiritual understanding. He tells them He uses parables to
keep the mysteries of the Kingdom of God from those who
are not of the Kingdom (verses 11 and 12). Then He makes
a powerful statement. He says the person who is able to
understand this parable can understand all the parables.

> **And he said unto them, Know ye not this parable? and how then will ye know all parables?**
>
> **Mark 4:13**

The Key

The key our Lord was giving His disciples is that *all truth is parallel.* Whatever is true in the natural realm will also be true in the spiritual. *Always look for the basic truth in the natural illustration, and you will find that same truth in its spiritual counterpart.* Remember, parables are nothing more than *parallels.*

The Seed Changes

Carefully notice that when Jesus restates the parable, the seed He speaks of in verse 14 is very different from the seed He used in verse 3. Jesus has replaced the agricultural seed with the Word. Obviously, the Word of God is not an agricultural seed. Words and seeds are different.

Here's another difference between the two stories of the parable. In the spiritual application, the sower doesn't plant the Word into the field. He sows it into the hearts of men. However, Jesus says the results of preaching the Word of God are *parallel* to the results of planting agricultural seed.

Now notice other parallels between the two stories. When the sower plants the Word of God into hearts that are like the wayside, Satan steals it (15). When he sows into stony hearts, no root system develops. At the first sign of persecution, the new convert gives up (16,17). When the sower plants the Word in a weed-infested heart, double-mindedness eventually causes the Word to lose its ability to bear fruit (18,19). However, when he sows the Word into hearts having good ground, harvest-proportion increase takes place, bringing forth thirty, sixty, and even a hundredfold (20).

When a Christian sows the Word, the same results take place as when a farmer sows the agricultural seed.

The Giver of Seed Power

Let me be very clear about this one thing. God is the only one who can give reproductive power.

> **And God said, Let the earth bring forth grass, the herb yielding seed, and the fruit tree yielding fruit after his kind, whose seed is in itself, upon the earth: and it was so.**
> **Genesis 1:11**

Evolution didn't give seed the power to reproduce, neither did the fictitious being called "Mother Nature."

Pay close attention to the hidden message of the second part of the parable. *God gives the power to reproduce to everything He calls a "seed."* With the power to reproduce also comes the potential of bringing forth thirty, sixty, and even hundredfold returns. However, harvest can happen only if you plant your seed in good ground.

Scripture tells us God has assigned seed-power to a number of things. Let's take a moment and look at just a few of them.

A Faith Seed

**. . . If ye have faith as a grain of mustard
seed . . .**
Matthew 17:20

Jesus gave harvest potential to faith when He called it a
"seed." Faith inside a good-ground heart responds the same
way the mustard seed does when a farmer sows it into good
ground. It starts out small, but it steadily grows. The
Apostle Paul tells us faith has potential for great increase.

. . . your *faith groweth exceedingly.* . . .
2 Thessalonians 1:3

A Kingdom Seed

Jesus tells us the Kingdom of God has seed-power.

**. . . Whereunto shall we liken [compare] the
kingdom of God? . . .**
It is like a grain of mustard seed. . . .
**But when it is sown, it groweth up, and
becometh greater than all herbs. . . .**
Mark 4:30-32

Think about it. The Kingdom of God that began as a
tiny mustard seed, has now grown literally to fill the whole
earth (Daniel 2:35). Surely we must classify that kind of
increase as a harvest proportion. God has given to *His
Kingdom,* the same power He has given to every
agricultural seed. Both faith and the Kingdom now have the
potential for mega-increase. Daniel tells of the expansive
power of the Kingdom of God.

**. . . the God of heaven set up a kingdom,
which shall never be destroyed . . . , but it shall**

> break in pieces and consume all these kingdoms,
> and it shall stand for ever.
> **Daniel 2:44**

Christian Seeds

> . . . if ye be Christ's, then are ye Abraham's
> seed. . . .
> **Galatians 3:29**

The entire Christian family is the spiritual seed of Abraham. God's Word said Abraham's seed would reproduce in harvest proportions. God said it would one day be as numerous as the stars of the sky.

> . . . [God] said, Look now toward heaven,
> and tell the stars, if thou be able to number
> them: and he said unto him, So shall thy seed be.
> **Genesis 15:5**

The multiplication of the Church is proof positive that the seed of Abraham has come forth in harvest proportions.

Jesus Is a Seed

When the disciples came saying certain Greeks desired to see Him, our Lord's response seemed strange. That is, unless you understand that He looked upon Himself as a seed. He understood Himself to be the beginning of a totally new species that would one day populate the entire earth.

> . . . there were certain Greeks. . . .
> The same came . . . to Philip . . . saying, Sir,
> we would see Jesus.

> **And Jesus answered them, saying, ...**
> **Verily, verily, I say unto you, Except a corn**
> **of wheat fall into the ground and die, it abideth**
> **alone: but if it die, it bringeth forth much fruit.**
> **John 12:20,21,23,24**

What a strange answer Jesus gives. Philip simply asks if some visitors from Greece might see Him. Notice that while their request has nothing to do with farming, our Lord gives them an agricultural answer. He says unless it falls into the earth, the seed abides alone.

Jesus Wasn't Showing Himself

To this day, our Lord's answer remains a mystery to most folks, for they don't understand it was impossible for anyone to *see* Jesus at that time. The only person He presented to the world was His Father. Keep in mind that only two chapters further, Jesus tells Philip that seeing Him is seeing His Father.

> **. . . he that hath seen me hath seen the**
> **Father. . . .**
> **John 14:9**

Our Lord's strange answer becomes clear when you understand that if they wanted to see Jesus, the Greeks would have to wait until the seed (Jesus) was planted into the earth. After His death, burial, and resurrection, Jesus would bring forth sons and daughters who would change from glory unto glory into His image (2 Corinthians 3:18). It would be the job of this new species (the born-again believers in Christ) to show Jesus to the world.

I hope you got it. When He spoke of the corn of wheat falling into the ground and dying, Jesus was speaking of

Himself. He was simply saying, "When I die and arise from the grave, I will bring forth many sons and daughters. They will show me [Jesus] to the world."

Money Given Into the Gospel

I have shown you God's ability to assign reproductive power to the things He calls "seed" to lay the groundwork for what I am about to share with you. God has given seed-power to the money you give into the gospel.

> **But remember this—if you give little, you will get little. A farmer who plants just a few seeds will get only a small crop, but if he plants much, he will reap much.**
> **2 Corinthians 9:6, TLB**

There you have it. When you give your money into the gospel, God automatically gives it seed-power. If you use wisdom and plant it in good-ground ministries, your money-seed has the potential of bringing forth a money harvest.

In the same way that the sower who sows agricultural seed has the right to look forward to a superabundant yield, the sower of spiritual seed has the right to look forward to a superabundant yield. The overwhelming truth of this parable is that *God automatically gives reproductive power (harvest potential) to everything He calls a "seed."*

This truth also pertains to your money. When you give your hard-earned money into the gospel, God looks at it as a *money-seed*, thereby giving it the potential for massive multiplication.

4

Those Within and Those Without

> . . . ye were sometimes darkness, but now
> are ye light. . . .
>
> **Ephesians 5:8**

In the verses between the two versions of the parable of the sower, Jesus gives us some other important information. He tells who actually makes the request for more information about the parable. The request comes from a previously obscure group of people.

Tradition leads us to believe it was the twelve apostles who asked. However, the language of verse 10 states something quite different.

> . . . they that were about him *with the twelve* asked of him the parable.
>
> **Mark 4:10**

At first it may seem as if I am splitting hairs. However, if you will allow me a brief moment, you will see there is more here than religion has taught us.

Inside the Circle

The Amplified Bible brings light to what Mark tells us.

> And He said to them, To you has been entrusted the mystery of the kingdom of God [that is, the secret counsels of God which are

31

hidden from the ungodly]; but to those outside [of our circle] everything becomes a parable.
Mark 4:11, Amplified

This interpretation tells us Jesus was speaking of Himself and His disciples (the twelve apostles and the other followers) as being in a circle. They were set apart from others. Jesus goes on to tell us there is also a group outside the circle. He refers to them as "them that are without." He says the mysteries of the Kingdom of God are exclusively for those with Him inside the circle. These mysteries are not public information, but private revelation.

> . . . Unto you [inside the circle] it is given to *know* the mystery of the kingdom of God: but unto them that are without, all these things are done in parables.
>
> **Mark 4:11**

A better translation of the word *know* would be *understand*. A group of people inside the circle with Jesus understands the mysteries of the Kingdom of God.

> . . . ye [little children of God] have an unction from the Holy One, and *ye know all things.*
> **1 John 2:20**

> . . . we [the brethren] have received . . . the spirit which is of God; *that we might know the things* that are freely given to us of God.
> **1 Corinthians 2:12**

Qualifying for Divine Understanding

Jesus tells us entering into the circle with Him is the first step to manifesting abundance through biblical principles. To enter our Lord's circle, you must depart from darkness and enter into the light. You must exit the realm of natural thinking and enter the realm of supernatural thinking. As a sinner, separated from God, you must come into fellowship with Him.

> . . . we are his workmanship, created in Christ Jesus unto good works. . . .
> . . . being in time past Gentiles in the flesh . . .
> . . . ye were without Christ, being aliens . . . and strangers . . . having no hope, and without God. . . .
> But now in Christ Jesus ye who sometimes were far off are made nigh by the blood of Christ.
> . . . that he might reconcile both [Jew and Gentile] unto God in one body by the cross . . .
> **Ephesians 2:10-13,16**

> . . . Except a man be born again, he cannot see [understand] the kingdom of God.
> **John 3:3**

Salvation takes place by accepting Jesus as your Savior. There are no two ways about it. God does not give the knowledge (understanding) of the mysteries of His Kingdom to those outside His circle. This wealth-gaining information comes only to those who are, as the Amplified Bible puts it, inside the circle. Only this group will be able to understand *Kingdom principles of increase.*

The Church

Our Lord speaks of a relationship between a group of people who are assembled with a leader. The advanced students (the twelve), or better said, the sub-leaders of the group surrounded the leader (Jesus). Another group consisting of less advanced students and relatively new followers surrounded those twelve. (This example is a good picture of the local church.)

I cannot overemphasize this truth. The first step in manifesting abundance by Kingdom principles is the new birth and membership in a proper New Testament church. Just being born again isn't enough. You must also be part of a church that will nurture and help you grow up in Christ.

Remember, this parable opens all parables to you. Now get this. Sowers are farmers, and farmers are *nurturers*. They nurture the tender sprouts carefully, taking care of them, feeding, watering, and protecting them until they come into full stature. In John 3:3, Jesus states that being born again allows you only to *see* the Kingdom of God. Something else must take place before you can *enter* and enjoy its benefits.

When will the Church learn that the *preaching* of the gospel only *saves* souls? The *teaching* of the Word of God *establishes* souls, causing them to experience the bountiful, new life God has for them.

Here's the bottom line. *Even if it falls into good ground, a seed cannot bring forth a harvest unless there is a farmer to nurture it into its full potential.* Neither can Christians bring forth the abundance God has planned for them without tender nurturing from a faithful pastor in a good local church.

There is a circle. It's called the "local church." Abundance by Kingdom principles comes only to those who grow to full stature by submitting to the environment and discipline of a proper local church.

5

Beyond Luke 6:38

... rightly dividing the word of truth.
2 Timothy 2:15

Tradition has made Luke 6:38 the favorite scripture at offering time.

> **Give, and it shall be given unto you; good measure, pressed down, and shaken together, and running over, shall men give into your bosom. For with the same measure that ye mete withal it shall be measured to you again.**
> **Luke 6:38**

Please remember that tradition can make the Word of God of no effect. (See Mark 7:13.)

Not a Harvest Concept

There is a major problem with using Luke 6:38 in connection with giving money into the gospel. This verse promises a very poor rate of increase. It doesn't even begin to reach harvest proportions. It promises only a pressed-down, running-over bushelful in return for each bushel you give.

Granted, it will be more than you gave. Yet, it will be a far cry from thirtyfold, sixtyfold, and a hundredfold. Why, the literal interpretation of Luke 6:38 doesn't even touch the hem of the garment of what Jesus proposes in Mark 4! The more you think about it, the more obvious it will become. Luke 6:38 does not speak of harvest-proportion returns.

No farmer would farm if he had to plant a bushel of corn to harvest one overflowing bushel of corn. It wouldn't be worth the effort for such a puny rate of return.

Harvest Is Not Natural

Strange as it may seem, harvest is not a natural event. Nowhere in nature does it occur without human intervention. Let me illustrate for you.

A grove of one hundred oak trees will yield literally thousands of acorns each year, but it won't bring forth thousands of additional oak trees each year. However, if a farmer gathers up all the acorns and places them in potting soil, carefully watering and nurturing them, the grove will produce thousands of oak trees each year.

You see, harvest is not a natural event. A human being has to take dominion over the natural rate of increase and force it into the wondrous dimensions we call "harvest."*

Jesus Teaches Mega-Increase

In Mark 4, Jesus clearly speaks of receiving in much greater proportions than just shaken down and running over. He speaks of thirty bushels for one, and sixty bushels

---

* *For more information on financial harvest, see **30-60-Hundredfold** by John Avanzini, published by Harrison House, Tulsa, OK 74153.*

for one, and even one hundred or more bushels for one. It is obvious that this kind of return would quickly lead to abundance.

What You Believe and Say

Scripture plainly teaches that you will have whatever you say and believe. Understanding this truth should make a big difference in the proportion of increase you will receive from future offerings.

> **For verily I say unto you, That whosoever shall *say* unto this mountain, Be thou removed, and be thou cast into the sea; and *shall not doubt* in his heart, but *shall believe* that those things which he *saith* shall come to pass; *he shall have whatsoever he saith.***
>
> **Mark 11:23**

As long as you confess a Luke 6:38 increase over your offerings, you will receive the meager rate of increase of that verse. Don't misunderstand. You will see an increase, but it will be no more than "... **pressed down, and shaken together, and running over. . . .**" However, if you will boldly begin to speak the thirtyfold, sixtyfold, and hundredfold return over your offerings, you will be one step closer to receiving harvest-proportion returns. If you speak and fully believe in your heart that what you say will come to pass, you will have whatever you say (Mark 11:23).

To move forward into this breakthrough, you will have to go beyond tradition into the realm of ". . . **rightly dividing the word of truth.**"

Study to show thyself approved . . . rightly dividing the word of truth.
2 Timothy 2:15

The Present Truth

Look at how perfectly this fresh revelation fits with the things the Holy Spirit has been revealing to the Body of Christ during the last few years. We have only recently begun to understand that money we give into the gospel is seed. However, we have hindered its potential by yoking it with the *snail's-pace increase* of Luke 6:38. Without realizing it, we have yoked the ox with the ass (Deuteronomy 22:10). In making this statement, I do not intend dishonor to the truth of Luke 6:38. I am merely showing how incompatible the slow growth rate of Luke 6:38 is, compared to the explosive potential existing in every seed.

Just imagine how much closer the Church would be to its goal of evangelizing the world if we had harnessed the truth of *seed-faith giving* with the high-powered potential of *harvest.*

Pull Out All the Stops

Why not just step out on the water of faith and go boldly where precious few have gone before? I challenge you to press on into the high ground that lies beyond the scant increase of Luke 6:38. Go all the way into harvest, where thirtyfold, sixtyfold, and a hundredfold are commonplace. Enter the land of *superabundance.*

Principle and Proportion

I am not suggesting you scrap Luke 6:38, for it plays an important part in every offering. It establishes the *principle of increase: Whatever you give, God will return to you increased.* However, Luke 6:38 does not begin to approach the full potential of return you can receive from your giving. The *proportion of increase* always depends upon the quality of the ground and the degree of human intervention.

If you plant in good ground and properly apply the laws of the harvest, your rate of increase can quickly grow into harvest proportions. It can easily reach thirtyfold, sixtyfold, or even a hundredfold.

The Measure of Your Return

The second thing Luke 6:38 establishes is that your measure of return will be in proportion with the measure of your giving.

If you plant an acre of wheat, you will not reap hundreds of acres of wheat. You will reap only the wheat your one acre brings forth. Paul reaffirms this truth when telling us the farmer who plants little will reap little, and if he plants much, he will reap much (2 Corinthians 9:6).

Scant giving will never produce mega-returns. If you give with a thimble, you will restrict God to giving back to you in thimblefuls. If you give with a teaspoon, you can receive only teaspoonfuls multiplied back to you. However, if you give by the truckload, God will give back to you in truckloads.

> ... For with the same measure that ye mete
> withal it shall be measured to you again.
> **Luke 6:38**

6

What Hundredfold Means

... abundantly above all that we ask or
think ...

Ephesians 3:20

For many years, my ministry has focused on the hundredfold return. This special anointing came to me during a very personal experience with God. During that encounter, He gave me specific instructions about speaking the hundredfold return over the offerings of His people. To the best of my ability, I have been faithful in doing as He said.*

During these years, many people have asked, "What does hundredfold really mean? Is it one hundred times? Is it 100 percent? Is it double? What does it really mean?"

For a long time the only answer I could give was that I didn't know exactly what it meant. I had to answer this way, because at the time, I had no specific revelation from the Lord about the numerical value of a hundredfold.

---

*   *For John Avanzini's personal testimony of how he received this special anointing from God, see **30-60-Hundredfold**, published by Harrison House, Tulsa, OK 74153.*

Best Possible

Recently God has increased His revelation to me in this area. Let's take a look at what He has shown me.

It is easy to understand what thirtyfold and sixtyfold mean. Thirtyfold means thirty times, and sixtyfold means sixty times. However, a hundredfold is much different. Notice that in telling the story of the sower, Jesus breaks the mathematical progression He uses after reaching sixtyfold. He progressed by thirty numbers at a time, until He went beyond sixtyfold. Then instead of adding another thirty to His count and coming to ninetyfold, He jumps forty numbers and ends with a hundredfold.

To understand what Jesus is doing, we must realize that one hundred is a unique number. It is the only one that can represent an indefinite amount of numbers. It can also mean complete, or *the best possible*.

In the classroom, one hundred represents the best possible score. If you were to take a test with one hundred questions, the best possible score would be one hundred. If the test had twenty-five questions, the best possible grade would not be twenty-five. It would still be one hundred. Let's go one step further. If a test had two hundred questions on it, the best possible grade would not be two hundred. It would still be one hundred.

More Than One Hundred Times

When it is planted in good ground, a little apple seed increases far more than one hundred times. One apple seed produces one apple tree. To determine the yield of the seed properly, you must count all the apple seeds the tree brings forth in its lifetime. It could be tens of thousands of seeds.

The average apple has about five seeds in it. We could safely conclude that if hundredfold meant only one hundred times, a hundredfold apple seed could bring forth only about twenty apples. The mathematics are as follows. Twenty apples times five apple seeds in each apple, equals one hundred apple seeds. However, we know that an apple tree can live many years, and it can produce thousands of apples. That information would mean that in the case of apple seeds, a hundredfold could easily equal tens of thousands of seeds. This information tells us that a hundredfold return can mean much more than just one hundred times.

Less Than One Hundred Times

If hundredfold had to mean exactly one hundred times, a cattle rancher could never experience the hundredfold return from a cow.

The average cow produces only one calf per year. Therefore, to bring forth one hundred calves would take one hundred years. That's longer than a cow's natural life span. As I understand it, a good breeder cow will bring forth about nine calves during her productive years. More than nine is considered exceptional. The best possible yield from a cow would be nine to thirteen calves. Therefore, hundredfold in the livestock industry (considering just the animals) would mean much less than one hundred times.

From these two illustrations, you can see that hundredfold can represent differing amounts of increase.

God has shown me through these examples that hundredfold would have to mean *the best possible yield.*

A Realtor Teaches Biblical Economics

Before you can consider something as the best possible yield, you must take circumstances into account. I personally came to understand this matter in a dramatic way. In 1981 my wife and I were moving away from Southern California. You can imagine our disappointment when we had to move before we sold our house. We left it in the hands of a capable realtor. No sooner had we moved than housing sales came to an abrupt halt.

After ten long months, the house finally sold. By then we had dropped our price a considerable amount. This loss had a real impact on me, because we had expected a fast, full-price sale. I remember rehearsing my disappointment to the Father. Little did I know how ungrateful my whining must have sounded to Him.

It was more than two years before my eyes opened to my ingratitude. Our California realtor and I were talking. He began to tell me what a miracle the sale of our house had been. It had been the only house in the area to sell during a two-year period. The local realtors were referring to the house we had sold as "the miracle house." They said it was the house God had sold for the preacher, when no other house was selling!

As soon as I was alone, I asked God to forgive me for being so ungrateful. I had murmured and complained *while God was giving me the best possible return.* I now realize we had experienced the hundredfold return. God had truly blessed us exceedingly, abundantly above anything the heathen had experienced under those same circumstances.

I have learned never to judge God's performance in my harvest until I have checked how the heathen come out with theirs. My God is the God of thirtyfold and sixtyfold, and no matter what the circumstances, He always gives me the best possible return! He always makes it a hundredfold!

Luke's Account

When you read the parable of the sower in Luke 8, the true meaning of a hundredfold becomes even clearer, for Luke doesn't even mention thirtyfold and sixtyfold.

> **And other fell on good ground, and sprang up, and bare fruit an hundredfold. . . .**
> **Luke 8:8**

When you compare Luke 8:8 with Mark 4:8, there is no question they are describing the same event. Mark's account says thirtyfold, sixtyfold, then a hundredfold. Luke says only hundredfold. This shows that hundredfold can mean any amount of increase.

My dear friend, I hope you can see that with the hundredfold return, it is possible for you to manifest the superabundance Jesus teaches in Mark 4. If you keep yourself in a position to receive *the best God has*, it won't take long for every promise of blessing and abundance in God's Word to become yours. It will be as the Scripture says.

> **. . . exceeding abundantly beyond all we ask or think. . .**
> **Ephesians 3:20**

7

The Candle Representing
the Spirit of Man

... walk in the spirit. ...
Galatians 5:16

To understand the revelation of Mark 4 properly, you must know exactly what Jesus meant in verse 21 when He spoke of the candle.

And he said unto them, Is a candle brought to be put under a bushel, or under a bed? and not to be set on a candlestick?
Mark 4:21

The Brick Wall

Not fully understanding this verse will block the flow of the whole fourth chapter for you. Remember that in the traditional interpretation, the candle presents a new subject that ends the teaching about receiving thirtyfold, sixtyfold, and a hundredfold.

In my early studies of this chapter, I kept thinking some evil conspirator must have committed the horrible sin of removing part of Mark's precious revelation. My spirit kept telling me our Lord had more to say about the wonderful realm of the hundredfold return. Why would He bring us to the threshold of mega-harvest (verses 8 and 20), and then without finishing the thought, just stop and begin a new discourse about beds, bushels, and candlesticks?

Harvest Proportions Would Change Everything

I just knew that if God's children could learn how to operate in the harvest principles of Mark 4, everything would quickly change for the Church. We would easily fund world missions. No longer would it be necessary to mortgage the gospel to build desperately needed church facilities. With a full explanation of how to manifest abundance, no Christian would ever have to say no to funding the end-time harvest.

All we needed was a step-by-step plan. Only a few more words, and the mega-return of Mark 4 would be ours. However, as I understood it, the chapter seemed to contain no practical, step-by-step instructions. Unless I was missing something, superabundant increase would have to go on existing only in parable form.

Divine Revelation Changes Things

How quickly things change when divine revelation comes! This is exactly what happened as I listened to Brother Copeland that cold January morning. He had just asked us to turn to Mark 4:21. No sooner had we turned than I realized he was about to comment on the brick-wall statement about the candle, bushel, and bed. I immediately focused all my attention on what he was saying.

I must say his next words were not the most profound I have ever heard. Brother Copeland simply stated that the candle spoken of in this verse was meant to have a figurative application. Jesus was using the candle to represent the spirit of man. To prove this point, he turned our attention to a verse in the Book of Proverbs.

48

The spirit of man **is the candle of the Lord. . . .**
Proverbs 20:27

The Brick Wall Came Down

Those were the last words of Brother Copeland's sermon I heard that day. Suddenly it all became clear to me. When He spoke of *placing the candle on the candle stand,* Jesus was not beginning a new thought. Verse 21 was not the brick wall I had thought. It is one of the most important steps a person must take to manifest harvest-proportion returns. Mega-harvest will be available only to those who will let their spirit control their life!

Revelation Stirs Revelation

By this time, the thoughts were coming so fast I barely had time to write them down. The spirit of revelation became so strong that most of what you find written in this book came to me in the next few minutes of that meeting.

Thank God, Mark 4 is no longer a series of disjointed thoughts! *It is a complete revelation of how the believer is to manifest harvest-size increase.*

We all know good ground is necessary for an abundant harvest in the natural realm; good ground is also necessary in the spiritual realm. To receive harvest-size returns, you must live a spirit-ruled life. The spirit-dominated life turns the natural heart (soul) into good ground.

Human Spirit, not the Holy Spirit

When He speaks of walking in the spirit in Mark 4 (putting the candle on the candlestick), our Lord is not instructing us to walk in the Holy Spirit. The biblical meaning of walking in the spirit is the process of conducting the affairs of your life under the direction and control of your own, reborn, reliable, human spirit. Jesus is saying that if you want mega-harvest, you must let your human spirit control your life. Spiritual harvest principles will not function in the life of a Christian whose soul or flesh dominates him. Harvest-proportion returns come only to Christians whose spirit-man rules.

Sowing Is Natural, Harvest Is Supernatural

Keep in mind that the sowing of seed is a natural process. However, the manifestation of increase from a seed is a spiritual process. Farmers are not all religious people. However, the Word of God declares that every time a farmer (saved or lost) has a harvest, two things take place. First, he sows a natural seed. Then supernatural intervention has to take place.

> **. . . So is the kingdom of God, as if a man**
> **should *cast seed into the ground;***
> **. . . and the seed should spring and grow up,**
> *he knoweth not how.*
> **Mark 4:26,27**

This verse tells us a miracle happens every time reproduction takes place. Notice the farmer plants the seed. However, the actual process causing the increase is beyond his ability to understand. It's supernatural! The Word of God says **". . . he knoweth not how."** God must activate the life-multiplying power in every seed if there is to be an increase. As smart as he considers himself, man still cannot manufacture a seed that will reproduce. Only God gives life.

A Three-Part Being

Scripture says you are made up of spirit, soul, and body.

> **. . . I pray God your whole *spirit* and *soul*
> and *body* be preserved blameless unto the
> coming of our Lord Jesus Christ.**
> **1 Thessalonians 5:23**

These three parts of your being are constantly striving for the leadership of your life. When the soulish portion of your being rules, your life becomes a process of manipulation that accomplishes only selfish goals. When your body rules, it will strive to accomplish only those things that please it. It is impossible, under the leadership of either the body or the soul, to live a Christ-centered life. The reason is that *"God is a Spirit. . ."* (John 4:24), and He chooses to communicate primarily with man's spirit. It is as the Psalmist says:

> **Deep calleth unto deep. . . .**
> **Psalm 42:7**

The Apostle John tells us that a person who will communicate with God must do so through his spirit.

> **. . . the true worshipers shall worship the
> Father in spirit and in truth: *for the Father
> seeketh such to worship him.***
> **God is a Spirit: and they that worship him
> must worship him *in spirit* and in truth.**
> **John 4:23,24**

For God to lead you into the understanding that brings forth abundance, you must be constantly communicating with Him. To communicate with God, your spirit must dominate your life.

51

Elihu, Job's friend, made an interesting statement about this communication. He pointed out that the spirit in man receives revelation from God.

> . . . there is a spirit in man: and the inspiration [breath] of the Almighty giveth them understanding.
>
> **Job 32:8**

Elihu is saying that the Spirit of God breathes understanding into the spirit of man. The reason is that the spirit of man corresponds to the substance of God.

> **God is a Spirit: and they that worship him must worship [communicate with] him in spirit and in truth.**
>
> **John 4:24**

God Wants to Talk to You

In Mark 4:21,22, Jesus tells of the need for the dominance of the spirit man (candle) and why He wants our spirits to dominate. Let me paraphrase these verses to clarify further what they are saying: The spirit of a man should not be hidden. It must be in the position of leadership over the man, because nothing is hidden that will not be manifest. Neither will anything be kept secret (Luke 8:17). So only the spiritually attuned ear will receive the wise counsel of God in manifesting abundance.

The breakthrough truth in these two verses quickly comes forth when we fully understand the candle. Placing your spirit man in control opens wide the door to understanding the whole chapter. All forty-one verses can now speak to us about the doctrine of Jesus, which is the miracle of seedtime and harvest.

8

Understanding and Receiving

**And ye shall know [understand] the truth,
and the truth [you understand] shall make you
free.**
John 8:32

The longer I am saved, the more I realize the need to understand the exact meanings of words. Nowhere is this understanding more important than in studying the Word of God.

The English language, as spoken by Americans, tends to change even more quickly than fashions in clothing do. It goes through an unending evolution that takes from, adds to, and even gives new meanings to its words.

Ears to Understand

The breakthrough truth I want to bring to you in this chapter deals with a word we find in Mark 4:9,23. The King James Version interprets it as *hear*. The Greek dictionary proves that translation of the word to be incomplete. Let's see how these two verses use it.

**. . . he said unto them, He that hath ears to
hear, let him *hear*.**
Mark 4:9

If any man have ears to *hear*, let him *hear*.
Mark 4:23

The original word is #191 in the Greek dictionary of Strong's concordance. It is the word *akouo*. The English word that accurately describes the intended meaning of this word in these verses is *understand,* meaning "to understand the thing you are hearing." In Matthew's account of the parable of the sower, the translators did translate it as *understand.*

> **When any one heareth the word of the kingdom, and *understandeth it not,* then cometh the wicked one, and catcheth away that which was sown in his heart. . . .**
> **Matthew 13:19**

Verse 23 says that the saint who *understands* what he hears will receive in harvest proportions.

> **But he that received seed into the good ground is he that *heareth* the word, *and understandeth* it; which also beareth fruit, and bringeth forth, some an hundredfold, some sixty, some thirty.**
> **Matthew 13:23**

When you apply this interpretation to the word in Mark 4:23, you see that our Lord is going on with His instructions about receiving the thirty, sixty, and hundredfold increase. See how clear it becomes when you use the word *understand* where the translators used the weaker *hear.*

> **If any man have ears to [understand], let him [understand].**
> **Mark 4:23**

Understanding Regulates Receiving

Now we can understand the intended meaning of verses 24 and 25. Our Lord warns us to be very careful with what we understand.

> . . . **Take heed what ye hear [understand]:**
> **with what measure ye mete, it shall be measured**
> **to you. . . .**
> **Mark 4:24**

The traditional interpretation of this verse has clouded the reason Jesus gave this warning. We have always compared the measure in verse 24 to the measure in Luke 6:38.

> . . . **For with the same measure that ye mete**
> **withal it shall be measured to you again.**
> **Luke 6:38**

Jesus is not speaking of the measure of Luke 6:38 in Mark 4:24. Keep in mind that He has been talking about *understanding,* so when the Lord says, ". . . **with what measure ye mete [or give], . . .**" He is not referring to the *amount* a person gives. The subject Jesus has been discussing establishes the measure of Mark 4:24. See a true revelation of verse 24 as I now show you the proper context.

> . . . **with what measure [of understanding]**
> **ye [give], it shall be measured to you. . . .**
> **Mark 4:24**

Paraphrased, it would be as follows: If any man has ears to understand, let him understand. He said again to them, be careful what you understand, because with whatever measure of *understanding* you do your giving, whatever you give will be measured back to you. Unto you who properly understand shall more be given.

Clearly our Lord is telling us that with this new insight, the more you understand about Him and His Word when you give, the greater your rate of return will be.

It's a Biblical Concept

The concept that your receiving will increase as your understanding increases is not new. Think for a moment, and you will realize that receiving according to your understanding pertains to all scriptural truth.

Understanding applies to the baptism in the Holy Ghost and speaking with other tongues. If you understand that God no longer gives the gift of tongues, you will find it difficult to receive the baptism of the Holy Ghost and your prayer language.

Your understanding also applies to divine healing. As long as you limit your understanding, and believe divine healing ended with the death of the twelve apostles, it will be extremely difficult for you to receive divine healing. Your lack of understanding God's ongoing plan of healing His children, will limit your ability to receive.

On the other hand, you can increase your understanding through studying God's Word, and recognize that God is the same yesterday, today, and forever (Hebrews 13:8). This increase in your understanding will enable you to believe that if He ever healed anyone, God is still healing people today. You can go even further and increase your understanding to know that when the Roman soldiers laid stripes on the back of Jesus, those stripes purchased healing for everyone. This simple growth in understanding will immediately allow you to receive healing. Not only that, but it will also qualify you for delivering God's healing power to others by the laying on of your own hands.

> . . . they [the saved] shall lay hands on the
> sick, and they shall recover.
> **Mark 16:18**

John the Beloved Taught It

What you just learned about increased understanding also brings increased prosperity. To see this truth, you must look with me at the prayer of the Apostle John.

> **Beloved, I wish [pray] above all things that
> thou mayest prosper and be in health, even *as
> thy soul prospereth.*
> 3 John 2**

Remember that your soul is your mind (intellect), will, and emotions. The word that best sums up these three parts of the soul is *understanding.* The main point of the Apostle John's prayer is not that you prosper, but that you prosper in direct ratio to your increase of understanding about prosperity.

Hear the condition he lays down for prospering and being in health.

> . . . as thy soul [understanding] prospereth
> [increases].
> **3 John 2**

Don't Give Up

When the promises of God seem difficult to receive, it is not the time to give up on them. It's time to turn to the Word of God and increase your understanding about the promise that is eluding you. Don't allow yourself to pass up even one promise from God. He wants you to have all of them. He makes this fact crystal clear by saying He doesn't tease us by offering promises He won't deliver.

> **... He isn't one to say "yes" when he means "no." He always does exactly what he says. He carries out and fulfills all of God's promises, no matter how many of them there are. ...**
> **2 Corinthians 1:19,20, TLB**

When receiving becomes difficult, don't give up. Just remember the instructions our Lord gives in Mark 4:24 where He says that with the same measure of understanding you do your giving, He will give back to you. Not only that, but keep in mind what the Apostle John said in 3 John 2. His top prayer was that your prosperity and health would increase as your understanding increases.

Twenty-Six Years of Observation

Twenty-six years of being a pastor have made me a student of human behavior. Time and again, I have seen two separate families in a church begin to tithe. They would both faithfully give their 10 percent each week.

Sometimes one family would experience an increase in their income, while the other family would see no change. After a while, the family who had seen no results would begin to complain and question the Word of God. They would eventually begin to accuse God of not prospering them as He did other tithers.

The truth is, there is nothing wrong with God. He is not a respecter of persons (Acts 10:34). His heart's desire is to prosper both families as much as they will allow.

Upon closer observation of such families, I have always found that one family prospered because they had a solid understanding of God's Word and what He expected from them. The solution for the other family was always simple. They had to get into God's Word and increase their understanding of His qualifications for receiving through the heaven their tithe had opened (Malachi 3:10). Most people wouldn't fully understand what I just said, but at least twenty-five things can immediately block the flow from heaven to a tither.*

It is imperative that you remember the words of our Lord. If you wish to increase your receiving, you must increase your understanding.

Remember: If any man has ears to understand, let him understand. He said again to them, be careful what you understand, because with whatever measure of *understanding* you do your giving, God will measure whatever you give, back to you. God will give more to you who properly understand (Mark 4:23,24 paraphrased).

---

*   *For more information on how to keep the windows of heaven open, see* It's Not Working, Brother John, *published by Harrison House, Tulsa, OK 74153.*

Farmer John

I want to close this chapter with a simple illustration. Just suppose I decided to move to a farm and make my living there for ten years. On this farm would be everything a farmer needed: tools, seed, fertilizer, books about farming, and information on the time and location of weekly classes on proper farming.

If I were to pay close attention to the lectures and totally believe what the textbook on farming said, I might have a harvest in the first year. Yet, if I did, it would no doubt be a limited one. If I were to continue to study and attend the lectures, faithfully applying every new thing I understood about farming, surely my harvest size would increase each year.

Why would this increase occur? It wouldn't be because attending lectures on farming would make me lucky. No, but the more I would study farming, the more my understanding of what to do would increase. The more I understood and followed good advice, the more harvest the good ground of that farm would be able to yield to me.

This same principle applies to your giving to God. With each bit of scriptural understanding you gain, you will automatically increase your ability to receive.

9

Jesus and the Wealth of the Wicked

... the wealth of the sinner is laid up for the just.
Proverbs 13:22

Every material possession God ever gave His children, came from the wicked. Even the wonderful Promised Land He gave Abraham was the bona fide possession of someone else. When Sarah died, Abraham buried her on the land God had given him. However, he had to pay cash for the burial site. While there is no question God had given him the land, Abraham had not yet taken possession of it.

God also took the wealth of the wicked Egyptians and gave it to His children when He brought them out of captivity. This same thing happened time after time throughout the Old Testament.

You don't have to go far in studying the Bible before you realize that God continually strips the wicked of their wealth and gives it to His children.

A good man leaveth an inheritance to his children's children: and the wealth of the sinner is laid up for the just.
Proverbs 13:22

He that by usury and unjust gain increaseth his substance, he shall gather it for him that will pity the poor.
Proverbs 28:8

> **For God giveth to a man that is good in his sight wisdom, and knowledge, and joy: but to the sinner he giveth travail, to gather and to heap up, that he may give to him that is good before God....**
>
> **Ecclesiastes 2:26**

> **This is the portion of a wicked man with God, and the heritage of oppressors, which they shall receive of the Almighty.**
> **Though he heap up silver as the dust, and prepare raiment as the clay;**
> **He may prepare it, but the just shall put it on, and the innocent shall divide the silver.**
>
> **Job 27:13,16-17**

These scriptures are crystal clear. They declare God's intention to give the wealth of the sinner to His righteous children. While everyone agrees the Old Testament teaches this truth, is it for us today?

It's for Today

With all respect to those who differ, Jesus does speak of transferring the wealth from the wicked to the just. One of the strongest instances is right here in Mark 4.

> **For he that *hath*, to him shall be given: and he that *hath not*, from him shall be taken even that which he hath.**
>
> **Mark 4:25**

Here Jesus is speaking of two groups, those who have and those who have not. To understand what the haves have and the have nots don't have, you must strictly adhere to the biblical context of this verse. Upon close examination, you will find that from verse 23 through 25, the subject never changes. Be careful, though, for Mark sometimes states the subject and sometimes implies it. However, it does not change. The subject remains *understanding.*

The most effective way to show you what our Lord is actually saying in verse 25 is to paraphrase once again, Mark 4:23-25: If any man has ears to understand, let him understand. He went on to say, Be careful what you understand, for with the same measure of understanding you do your giving, God will measure your return back to you. The more understanding you have, the greater your return will be, for he who has *understanding* will receive, and he who doesn't have *understanding,* even the wealth he has will be taken from him.

When these verses are written out in this way, it is easy to see that our Lord is speaking of removing the possessions of one group, and giving them to the other. He identifies one group as having understanding, and the other as not having it.

In Mark 4:10-12, our Lord makes it clear who understands and who doesn't. When He is alone with the disciples, they ask about the meaning of the parable of the sower. He tells them they (the children of God) can know (understand) the mysteries of the Kingdom of God, but outsiders (the children of darkness) can't know (understand) them. The twelfth verse puts it plainly.

> **That seeing they may see, and not perceive
> [understand the things they see]; and hearing
> they may hear, and not understand. . . .**
> **Mark 4:12**

Jesus simply says He will give the possessions of those who don't understand the Kingdom of God (the wicked) to those who do understand it (those who are righteous in His sight). In Mark 4:25, Jesus is actually repeating the second part of Proverbs 13:22.

> ... **the wealth of the sinner is laid up for the just.**
>
> **Proverbs 13:22**

How clear these words become when we understand Mark 4:23-25 in its scriptural context! Jesus is simply telling us where God is temporarily storing the abundance He wants to give us. It is now in the hands of the wicked. They have it stacked up together and rusting, awaiting the end of time when God will redistribute it to His children.

> **Go to now, ye rich men, weep and howl for your miseries that shall come upon you.**
>
> **Your riches are corrupted, and your garments are motheaten.**
>
> **Your gold and silver is cankered; and the rust of them shall be a witness against you, and shall eat your flesh as it were fire.** *Ye have heaped treasure together for the last days.*
>
> **James 5:1-3**

God plans to give us the wealth the wicked now possess.

Two Other Places

Jesus plainly states in two other places that God will give the wealth of the wicked to the just. One is in the sixth chapter of Matthew where He tells us of the benefits of seeking first His Kingdom.

> **... seek ye first the kingdom of God, and his righteousness; and all *these things* shall be added unto you.**
> **Matthew 6:33**

With close examination of the context of this verse, you will find that Jesus promises to add to those who seek first the Kingdom of God and His righteousness, the very same things the Gentiles (sinners) are seeking to stack up.

> **(For after all these things do the Gentiles seek:) ...**
> **But seek ye first the kingdom of God, and his righteousness; and all these things shall be added unto you.**
> **Matthew 6:32,33**

Jesus is saying: Seek first the Kingdom of God and His righteousness, and all the things the sinners are stacking up, God will subtract from them and add to you.

Jesus also declares that God will give the wealth of the wicked to the just in Matthew 25, in the parable about the talents. If you remember, the master gave five talents to one servant, two talents to another, and one to the last. Two of these servants were faithful to obey the master and increase their talents. However, the third one hid his talent in the ground. When he came to reckon with this disobedient servant, the master said:

> **... Thou *wicked* and slothful servant ....**
> **Take therefore the talent from him, and give it unto him which hath ten talents.**
> **Matthew 25:26,28**

Take the money from the wicked servant, and give it to the obedient servant!

Thank God, the mega-wealth the wicked now possess is once again ready to change hands. No longer will it stagnate in their treasure houses. It is even now ready for redistribution among the informed children of God.

Wealth Never Lies in the Streets

These words from the lips of our Lord bring much credibility to the message of manifesting superabundance, for everyone knows that wealth never lies in the streets. It's always in someone's possession. God will simply take it from the wicked as He has done in times past, and give it to His children. Remember, if He has done it before, you can depend upon His doing it again (Hebrews 13:8). This situation becomes clear, especially when we see our Lord's words in the true context of Mark 4.

There is more wealth in the world today than ever before. It's out there right now, waiting for that special end-time group of Christians who will understand enough about biblical economics to acquire and use it.

10

A Process Not an Event

To every thing there is a season, and a
time. . . .

Ecclesiastes 3:1

In Mark 4:26-28 notice how smoothly our Lord
changes the subject from transferring the wealth from the
wicked to the the just, to the timing involved in manifesting
the wealth transfer.

Jesus tells us that abundance by biblical principles
comes in the same way the farmer's harvest does. We all
know that bringing a seed to harvest is never an
instantaneous event. It always comes through a time-
consuming process.

*God's abundant supply comes from a lifestyle of
sowing that steadily progresses from stage to stage.* Each
time of sowing brings more abundance, until the final
phase, which is exceedingly abundant, above all you can
ask or think (Ephesians 3:20).

The Process

Notice Jesus again uses a parable to illustrate the time
needed for manifesting abundance.

And He said, The kingdom of God is like a
man who scatters seed upon the ground,

> **And then continues sleeping and rising
> night and day while the seed sprouts and grows
> and increases—he knows not how.**
>
> **The earth produces [acting] by itself—first
> the blade, then the ear, then the full grain in the
> ear.**
>
> **Mark 4:26-28, Amplified**

It is evident from these verses that Jesus is not
speaking of the timing associated with the world's method
of accumulating abundance. In the uncertain system of this
world, everyone tries to make it as fast as he can. Words
such as *windfalls, ripoffs,* and *killings* are common in the
financial realm of darkness. However, we are in the world,
but not of the world (John 17:16). Our Lord is not inviting
us to participate in the flawed process of natural wealth
accumulation. Instead, He is showing us His unfailing
principles of supernatural wealth accumulation.

> **While the earth remaineth, seedtime and
> harvest ... shall not cease.**
>
> **Genesis 8:22**

The Timing

In Mark 4:26-28, Jesus is describing the time needed
for manifesting harvest-proportion increases. Hear it
again. You must not only sow your seed into the good
ground of the gospel, but you must also allow time to
pass. The farmer sleeps and rises a number of times
before his seed progresses to the next stage. During this
time, the sprouts appear, grow, and increase. It is a
process, not an event. It takes time, for many nights and
days pass as the seed develops.

Three Definite Periods

Three distinct time periods divide the process leading to harvest. Our Lord calls them "the blade," "the ear," and "the full corn in the ear." It is important to understand these three stages of growth, for they prepare you for the definite changes that must take place in the seed as it moves toward harvest. Without clear understanding, the first two stages could cause you to become discouraged, and you could miss the harvest. However, when you understand them, these stages assure you that the seed is properly progressing. Once again, it depends on your understanding.

The Blade

After the farmer sows it, his seed is completely out of his control. For a while it seems as if nothing is going to happen. The field looks empty for many days. During this barren season, patience is necessary.

> ... be ... followers [imitators] of them who
> through faith and patience inherit the promises.
> **Hebrews 6:12**

For those who have patience, by and by a change takes place. The blade breaks through the soil, and everything takes on a new perspective. The process is working and harvest is coming. However, blade time can be detrimental to harvest, for it brings the temptation to end the whole process by consuming the sprouts.

The Spiritual Realm

In the spiritual application of blade time, this same danger exists. As soon as you experience the first increase from giving, you may be tempted to spend it all on your personal needs and desires.

No doubt the disciples faced this same kind of temptation during the miracle feedings our Lord performed. Just think of the temptation when they saw fish and loaves rapidly multiplying in their hands. How tempting it must have been to set aside a few choice fish and some nice, fresh loaves for their own personal use.

Thank God, they didn't give in to their basic instincts, for when the fish and loaves stopped multiplying in their hands, our Lord had not forgotten them. There were twelve large basketfuls left over (Mark 6:35-44). Their patience brought them more than they could have hidden away while distributing the loaves and fishes.

Now here it is in a nutshell. When the first signs of financial increase show up, don't stop giving. Just keep on planting and replanting. Make sure each successive time of sowing contains a greater portion of each new harvest.

The blade stage is to be a time of hope, not a season of foolishly eating up the sprouts. Let each sprout grow into a full harvest. Remember, harvesting sprouts brings nothing more than a Luke 6:38 return. It will be only a little bit more than you planted. However, if your faith, hope, and patience can prevail, allowing your seed to reach its full potential, God's Word says it can yield thirtyfold, sixtyfold, and even a hundredfold.

Don't be like Judas who didn't have the faith and patience to wait for the manifestation of the Kingdom of

God. His desire for immediate gratification caused him to sell our Lord for a mere thirty pieces of silver, which were nothing more than sprouts compared to the value of everlasting life. Instead, you should be like Father Abraham who patiently waited for God to deliver the full measure of everything He had promised him.

> **And so, after he had patiently endured, *he obtained* the promise.**
> **Hebrews 6:15**

Blade time is the wrong time to put in the sickle and reap.

Stalk Time

The King James Version translates our Lord's words as "**. . . then the ear . . .**" (Mark 4:28). I'd like to call it "stalk time." It is after the tender sprout becomes a rough, rigid stalk. This phase of development seems the longest to the farmer. Not only does it take a long time, but the crop starts looking as if it has died.

We Looked Like Fools

I can personally testify to the difficulty that goes with this waiting time, for my wife and I have been through it. Waiting caused us to look like fools to our family. It was as if we were standing still financially. Everyone seemed to be doing better than we were. We gave and gave, and then just gave some more. However, no matter how much we gave, we just didn't seem to be getting ahead, as the others in our family were. All we could see were stalks. Oh, yes! God met our needs, but we didn't seem to be accumulating anything.

During this period of time, we learned what Christians mean when they say, "We know that we know that we know." We just wouldn't give up, because God's Word kept telling us our God would come through.

Stalk time separates believers who know God's Word is true from those who *only hope His Word is true*. Most Christians who give up and go back to the economic system of the world, do so during stalk time. I wish it were possible to go immediately from blade time to harvest time. However, God in His infinite wisdom has not chosen to make it that way. Every Christian who will walk in the full manifestation of harvest will have to go patiently through the dry season of stalk time.

Harvest Time

How wonderful it is when the farmer thrusts in the sickle and takes the harvest! The exhilaration of reaping is so totally satisfying that the farmer sows again and again toward even bigger harvests. It is an experience beyond description. This glorious feeling is especially wonderful when it comes in the financial realm. You have unspeakable joy when the fear of insufficiency is gone from your life. You can give freely again and again, knowing your Father's Word is true, and it will never fail you.

> . . . my God shall supply all your need
> according to his riches in glory by Christ Jesus.
> Philippians 4:19

You have great comfort when you know that shortage can no longer come near your dwelling. Your supply no longer depends on the flawed system of the world. It depends on the unfailing promise of God that says, **"While** the earth remaineth, seedtime and harvest . . . shall not cease" (Genesis 8:22).

Even as I write this book, my wife and I are experiencing the harvest season. While the world stands at the edge of recession and economic meltdown, we are full of hope, expecting the ongoing increase of God's abundant supply.

Not an Event

Remember, the manifesting of superabundance in the economy of God is never an instantaneous event. It is a time-consuming process. However, rest assured that the manifestation of thirty, sixty, and even a hundredfold will be worth the time it takes. When it comes to full maturity, your heaven-sent harvest will be as the Scripture says, exceeding abundantly, above all you can ask or think (Ephesians 3:20).

True Christianity Is Expensive

When you properly operate it, your Christianity quickly becomes the most expensive lifestyle a human being can undertake. I say this because in its purest form, the gospel instructs us to feed the hungry (Matthew 25:35-45). Notice it doesn't talk about just a few hungry people, but all the hungry. Now that's expensive business. The gospel also instructs us to clothe the naked. That doesn't mean just a few of the naked, but all of them. Once again, we are talking about big money. To demonstrate true Christianity, we must literally go into all the world and preach the good news to every creature. Every creature means every last one of them (Mark 16:15).

It doesn't take a genius to understand that if we feed all the hungry, clothe all the naked, and evangelize the lost, the cost of doing it correctly will make it the most expensive venture we have ever undertaken.

Divine Enabling

When He placed the tremendous responsibility of world evangelism upon His Church, the Lord made Himself responsible for supplying the resources we would need to accomplish the task. Hear the angel Gabriel as he reassures us of this fact.

> **. . . no word from God shall be without power or impossible of fulfillment.**
> **Luke 1:37, Amplified**

The Bible tells us God has already approved and set aside all the supply we need to fulfill godliness. Hear the apostle as he reaffirms the availability of this exceeding abundance.

> **According as his divine power hath given unto us all things that pertain unto life and godliness, through *the knowledge* [understanding] of him that hath called us to glory and virtue.**
> **2 Peter 1:3**

Thank God, the Church doesn't have to depend on the worldly methods of increasing wealth. God has chosen the unfailing principles of seedtime and harvest to provide the wealth we need to fulfill the Great Commission.

> **While the earth remaineth, seedtime and harvest . . . shall not cease.**
> **Genesis 8:22**

11

The Lord of the Harvest

> . . . the seed sprouts and grows and
> increases—he knows not how.
> Mark 4:27, Amplified

Our Lord makes a very important statement when He says the farmer does not know how the seed becomes a plant. He isn't saying the farmer has no knowledge of the processes that take place in transforming a seed into a plant. He is simply saying the farmer does not have the ability to duplicate the process.

If they had ten billion dollars to spend, the professors of the most advanced agricultural university in the world could not design, engineer, or produce a seed that could bring forth a living plant. Man just cannot make a seed. He can enhance it so that it produces more. He can genetically alter a seed, bringing forth a mutation. However, he cannot start with raw materials and produce a seed from scratch, for a seed contains life, and only God can give life.

> All things were made by him; and without
> him was not any thing made that was made.
> In him was life. . . .
> John 1:3,4

When you fully understand it, this truth will become perfectly reasonable to you: God should share in your harvests, for there is never a harvest unless God does His part. He gives the power of reproduction to the seeds you plant. Yes, the farmer must work hard if he expects an abundant harvest. He must also plant in good soil. However, unless God does His part, there will never, under any circumstances, be a harvest.

> . . . it was God, not we, who made the
> garden grow. . . .
> 1 Corinthians 3:6, TLB

Scripture clearly teaches that man is to reward the ox for plowing, and that the laborer is worthy of his hire (pay). Just as the farmer deserves his portion of the increase, God is entitled to His share of everything that increases upon the earth, for He is the main contributor in all increase. Thank God we don't have to guess how much His efforts are worth! He has already established the value of His contribution to every increase. He says His part will be 10 percent (the tithe).

> Honor the Lord with thy substance, and
> with the firstfruits of all thine increase.
> Proverbs 3:9

> Thou shalt truly tithe all the increase of thy
> seed, that the field bringeth forth year by year.
> Deuteronomy 14:22

> . . . all the tithe of the land, whether of the
> seed of the land, or of the fruit of the tree, is the
> Lord's: it is holy unto the Lord.
> Leviticus 27:30

The Scripture is clear that God believes 10 percent of all the increase of the earth is His. Ten percent is not a gift to Him. Neither is it a tax. Rather, it is His appointed portion for His part in bringing forth increase.

No matter what the endeavor, if there is increase, God has a part in it. Whether it be the woodsman who sells a tree he has cut down, or the security guard who draws wages for forty hours of work, Jehovah God plays a part in every person's increase. The woodsman owes God the tithe because he sold God's tree. The security guard owes 10 percent of his wages because God allowed him the forty hours he spent earning his wage.

When He said the farmer did not know how the seed grew into a plant, our Lord was actually stating that Jehovah God makes an invaluable contribution to everything that increases. Therefore, God must receive His tithe.

Hear it, and hear it well. There will be no manifestation of abundance by biblical principles unless you pay the tithe that keeps heaven open over your seed (finances).

12

Growing Upward

. . . as long as he sought the Lord, God
made him to prosper.

2 Chronicles 26:5

The requirement Jesus speaks of next is single-mindedness. The person successful in harvest will keep his finances involved in the business of the Kingdom of God. Our Lord tells us the seed growing into harvest proportions *must continually grow upward.*

. . . when it is sown, it groweth up. . . .
Mark 4:32

Distraction Brings Disaster

How often I have seen people in a desperate season of their lives, call upon the mercy of God for help! I am primarily speaking of those who said they would either receive a financial miracle or perish. When people reach this point, their giving to God usually comes as a last resort, but they pledge and pay. Then when the promised abundance starts coming, they foolishly turn their finances away from funding the gospel and begin, once again, looking to worldly schemes for their increase.

Others hear their pastor speak from the Word of God about giving and receiving. Out of simple obedience, they begin to follow his instructions which soon lead them to experience God's promised increase. Everything goes well until their financial assets become substantial. Then, all of a sudden, they begin to feel that their wealth has become too great to trust to the advice of a mere pastor. Now they need tax consultants and financial planners.

Step by step, they leave off tithing and giving until they do little more than tip God. How subtly the devil works when he redirects a person's financial affairs!

If your finances ever lose their upward focus, they will also lose their divine empowerment. Tax consultants and financial planners have their place in the lives of God's children. Nevertheless, before they can properly help you, these experts must understand that your source is the God of heaven. You must inform them it is absolutely necessary for you to have an open heaven, meaning that tithes and offerings are not optional in your portfolio. You must let them know that no investment can ever come before your tithe and generous offerings. Make it plain. Even if it means passing up the deal of the century, you will not go one week without tithing.

Caught in the Trap

So many times I have seen the children of God drawn away from the manifestation of abundance because someone suddenly came up with a great deal. It always sounds so simple. All they have to do is give up tithing and giving offerings for six short months. I can still hear them saying, "Trust me, Pastor. When this deal comes through, I will single-handedly fund the vision for the whole church."

After twenty-six years as a pastor, I can say without hesitation that I have never seen one of these God-robbing deals work out. That's not all. Not only did the deals go bad, but the embarrassment these folks suffered drove most of them out of the Church and away from their God.

Even if you can buy the Empire State Building for 20 percent of its appraised value, if making the deal involves having to say no to God in one offering, *pass up the deal!*

Remember, the financial plan that grows into full harvest proportions is one that continually grows upward. It never gets out of focus with God's purpose.

> **... thou shalt remember the Lord thy God:**
> **for it is he that giveth thee power to get wealth,**
> ***that he may establish* his covenant which he**
> **sware unto thy fathers, as it is this day.**
> **Deuteronomy 8:18**

Don't worry about missing out on the good life. As long as you fulfill God's purpose in your giving, God will loose abundance into your hands.

Faithful Stewards Are Blessed

In Matthew 25:14-46, Jesus tells us how He will bless His trustworthy stewards. Their faithfulness in financial matters will cause Him to increase their belongings. He says the Kingdom of God is as a man who is going to travel into a far country who first calls his own servants (stewards) to him. He doesn't call someone else's servants, but his own. Then Jesus says this man delivers to these stewards various amounts of his money. (A talent is a measure of money.) He gives one five talents; another, two, and the third, one.

Notice carefully that the master gives money to his stewards. Then they redistribute the wealth of their master as he directs them.

In the parable, the steward with five talents goes about his master's business and gains five more talents. Verses 19-21 tell us that when he reckons with him, the master generously rewards his steward for his faithfulness. He says to him, "Well done, good and faithful servant. You have faithfully kept your focus on my business. Because you have diligently promoted and expanded that which is mine, I am now going to expand that which is yours by making you ruler over many things" (Matthew 25:21 paraphrased).

I believe with all my heart that faithful stewards who constantly focus their attention on funding the end-time harvest will come into superabundance. This plan of seedtime and harvest will not let you down if you don't let it down. From personal experience, I can now bear witness to the fact that great abundance comes to those who constantly give into the gospel of Jesus Christ.

The Socially Correct Mistake

I have seen one more disturbing trend among many who attempt to prosper by biblical principles. It is a subtle thing that happens almost without notice.

Because of the evangelical emphasis of most faith churches, many of their converts come from the lower economic levels of society. As they begin to prosper, these folks are cast in with a part of society unfamiliar to them. As they progress up the corporate ladder, they begin to associate with the crowd the world calls "the right people," "the movers and the shakers," if you please. This part of society wants to be with the people who can make things happen for them. They are very conscious of projecting the right image.

All too often when they move up into higher social circles, these good, common, down-to-earth people begin to feel that the wrong social crowd attends their faith church. They feel pressure to get into the church where the right people go, people who can help them the most in their careers.

I am reminded of the story about the corporate executive who faithfully attended an evangelical church. He was always witnessing and bringing visitors to church. One day he brought the Chief Executive Officer (CEO) of his Fortune 500 corporation. As they were leaving, he asked him how he had enjoyed the pastor's sermon. The boss ignored his question, so he asked again. "Tell me, how did you like my pastor's sermon?"

The visiting executive finally answered, "It was interesting, but his grammar was far from perfect. How in the world can you, a man in top management in the largest corporation in this city, stand to hear a man you call 'pastor' say he 'seed' something?"

The church member swallowed and replied, "I don't particularly enjoy listening to incorrect grammar. But, I would rather have a pastor who says he 'seed' something when he actually saw it, than have a polished pastor who says he saw something when he didn't really see anything."

Please note I am not defending poor grammar. However, if you have to choose between a real man of God who lacks polish and a hireling who speaks the king's English, always choose the man of God.

How terrible this attitude is, for most of the time these so-called "right" churches, or socially acceptable churches, lack the power of the Holy Ghost. They also lack the good faith teaching so necessary to those who wish to continue prospering in the economy of God. Sad to say, but these elite churches are usually not good ground. Hear me, and hear me well. When a Christian stops giving into good ground, his seed will stop bringing forth harvest proportions.

Time after time these misguided folks move their membership from the churches that won them to Christ, to the socially acceptable churches in their community. They find a place where the pastor is a bit more polished, and where the primary spiritual statement is rich woods, stained glass, and unique architecture. These misguided folks take their focus off the upward growth of their seed, and as always, the power of God departs.

Whatever you do, when you start on the road of biblical economics, keep your money involved in a live church dedicated to evangelism. Be vigilant, and see to it that tithing and giving offerings to God are the main uses for your money. Always keep in mind that you are a steward of God, and as a steward, God requires you to be faithful.

> ... it is required in stewards, that a man be found faithful.
>
> **1 Corinthians 4:2**

13

The Man of God

Society has created many prestigious positions. They range from king, queen, and president, all the way down to chief dogcatcher and sanitary engineer. However, there is a greater office than any of these, and it is not man-made. It is the office of the pastor.

The office of pastor is greatly misunderstood. Even among church members, most do not place the proper importance on their pastor's words. They don't look at them as having any special long-term benefit or consequence. Many Christians feel their pastor only makes suggestions to which they may or may not choose to pay attention. This attitude about the man of God is a grave mistake, for the Word of God says your pastor will be present with you on the most important day of your life. He will stand with you in the judgment.

> **Obey them that have the rule over you, and submit yourselves: for they watch for your souls, *as they that must give account,* that they may do it with joy, and not with grief: for that is unprofitable for you.**
> **Hebrews 13:17**

Never Over-speeding the Sheep

With the 33rd verse, Mark begins to tell us of the pastoral relationship Jesus had with His disciples.

> **And with many such parables spake he the**
> **word unto them,** *as they were able to hear it.*
> **Mark 4:33**

Notice that Jesus did not set a grueling pace for His disciples in their training program. Instead, He set the pace of His teaching by their ability to understand Him.

> **... as they were able to hear [understand] it.**
> **Mark 4:33**

Real men and women of God will be careful about the feeding and activities of their church members. They won't let just anyone minister to the congregation. They will allow only those who have God's Word for their church.

Multi-Level Ministering

The insight Mark gives about the qualifications of a proper pastor expands with each sentence. Next he tells us that a proper pastor operates his church with two levels of teaching. He presents one level to the general assembly.

> **But without a parable spake he not unto**
> **them....**
> **Mark 4:34**

He also has deeper teaching for the more advanced students in the inner circle. This teaching always takes place away from the general assembly. These sessions are deeper-truth believers' meetings. Our Lord chose these times to make obscure things clear to His disciples.

> **... [Jesus]** *expounded* **all things to his**
> **disciples.**
> **Mark 4:34**

In those private teaching sessions, Jesus compared the parables He took from the natural realm with the spiritual truths they represented. In this way, He explained the truth the parables held. This form of teaching planted each truth into the memories of his disciples, by attaching it to a natural phenomenon familiar to them.

The Heart of the Pastor

Let's go a bit deeper by comparing the pastor's heart (Jacob) with one who has a natural gift of leadership (Esau). In Genesis 33 Jacob and Esau are ready to leave the encampment where they reconciled their differences. Esau proposes to go first and set the pace for their journey.

> **And he [Esau] said, Let us take our journey, and let us go, and I will go before thee.**
> **Genesis 33:12**

Jacob's answer typifies the heart of the true pastor.

> **And [Jacob] said unto him, My lord knoweth that the children are tender, and the flocks and herds with young are with me: and if men should overdrive them one day, all the flock will die.**
> **Let my lord, I pray thee, pass over before his servant: and I will lead on softly, according as the cattle that goeth before me and the children be able to endure, until I come unto my lord unto Seir.**
> **Genesis 33:13,14**

Notice that Esau didn't allow himself to be bothered with flocks and precious children as Jacob did. Verse 1 tells us he allowed no little ones to go with him. His troops were all grown men.

> **. . . Esau came, and with him four hundred men. . . .**
>
> **Genesis 33:1**

I never read this portion of Scripture without thinking of the true shepherd's heart. His forward progress does not depend upon the goal he has set for his ministry. It depends on the well-being of the flocks and herds (people) with him.

After they reconciled their differences, both Esau and Jacob planned to go to the region of Seir. However, their methods of getting there differed greatly. Esau said, "Let's go! I'll lead! We'll get there fast!"

Jacob said, "No, I can't speed up the little ones, or they will all die."

Esau left and made one big push that took him all the way to Seir. Jacob's trip would be a much longer journey.

> **. . . [Esau,] you go on ahead of us and we'll follow at our own pace and meet you at Seir.**
> **So Esau started back to Seir that same day. Meanwhile Jacob and his household went as far as Succoth. There he built himself a camp, with pens for his flocks and herds. (That is why the place is called Succoth, meaning "huts.")**
> **Genesis 33:14,17, TLB**

A proper pastor will *lead* the flock. He will never *drive* them. A real pastor will give up his own timetable and gear his schedule to the ability of his flock to follow. He must nurture them, allowing their rate of progress to become his rate of leadership. Since Jesus is the pattern pastor, true pastors must allow the Lord's way of doing things to become their way of doing things.

A Friend Closer Than a Brother

Next, our Lord exemplifies an important aspect of pastoring. When the storm arises and His disciples awaken Him, He doesn't read them the riot act for disturbing His rest. Neither does He make a spectacle of them because of their poor confession ("**. . . we perish!**"). He simply rises up and comforts them by stilling the storm.

A real pastor will teach his flock to have faith and speak a proper confession. He will not chide the weaker ones who cannot keep up the pace; he will help them by making their journey as comfortable as possible. This attitude is just the opposite of how the world system teaches progress. The world teaches the survival of the fittest. That's not the way it is with God. In God's Kingdom, the strongest ones serve all and save even the weakest.

> . . . Jesus called them unto him, and said, Ye know that the princes of the Gentiles exercise dominion over them, and they that are great exercise authority upon them.
> But it shall not be so among you: but whosoever will be great among you, let him be your minister;
> And whosoever will be chief among you, let him be your servant:
> Even as the Son of man came *not to be ministered unto, but to minister.* . . .
> **Matthew 20:25-28**

> How think ye? if a man have an hundred sheep, and one of them be gone astray, doth he not leave the ninety and nine, and goeth into the

mountains, and seeketh that which is gone astray?

Even so it is not the will of your Father which is in heaven, that one of these little ones should perish.

Matthew 18:12,14

A Father Not a Grandfather

One last thing about the true pastor is that he has a father's heart, not a grandfather's heart. Grandfathers tend to spoil children. They let them get away with bad behavior without any admonition. Such is not so with a true pastor. After the danger is past, he deals firmly with the shortcomings of his people.

If you notice, our Lord stills the storm and gently delivers the disciples to the other side of the lake. Afterwards, He deals with the problem that took place.

And he said unto them, Why are ye so fearful? how is it that ye have no faith?

Mark 4:40

They didn't need pity. They needed a lesson on faith. Notice that He had not said, "Let's go perish" in verse 35; He had said, **". . . Let us pass over unto the other side."** The disciples had exercised no faith in His words.

A true pastor will admonish and teach his flock each time their faith fails, until every member of the church is able to stand boldly on every word of God.

The person who wants to manifest abundance by the biblical principles of increase must have a real pastor. Such a pastor is not an option, but a necessity.

14

The Conclusion

I hope you can now see that Mark 4 is not the chopped up, disjointed array of unrelated thoughts tradition portrays. Instead it is a single revelation that continues uninterrupted, for forty-one verses. It is our Lord's magnificent teaching on the process of manifesting abundance.

Mark 4 begins with the bold statement that Jesus is going to declare His doctrine. This chapter simply illustrates a sower planting his seed. The full spiritual meaning of the chapter is that God gives potential for harvest-proportion increase to anything He calls "a seed."

Our Lord then teaches that all truth is parallel. Whatever is true in the natural world is also true in the spiritual world. He shows us that parables are nothing more than parallels.

Verse 21 seemed to be a barrier, switching the subject to candles, bushels, and beds. However, it actually turns out to be the criterion for participating in the exceeding abundance above all we can ask or think (Ephesians 3:20). Yes, you must place your spirit-man on the candlestick. Your spirit must rule, or God will not make the secrets of Kingdom increase known to you.

Then Mark reveals that we must understand God's principles of increase before we can take over the wealth of this world (Proverbs 13:22). Warning lights go on, and we find that God's way of abundance is not a get-rich-quick scheme. In God's way, growth comes slowly. It comes first as a blade, then the stalk, then the harvest.

Warning lights come on again as Jesus instructs us to keep our focus ever upward. If we take our eyes off Kingdom principles, we soon lose God's "**. . . power to get wealth . . .**" (Deuteronomy 8:18).

Finally comes the clear teaching of the pastor and the church in the matter of the storm. It is impossible to maximize harvest increase without the guidance of a true pastor.

When you put all these lessons together with other things our Lord will reveal to you from Mark 4, life will begin to progress, as the prophet said it would.

> **Behold, the days come, saith the Lord, that the plowman shall overtake the reaper, and the treader of grapes him that soweth seed. . . .**
> **Amos 9:13**

You will have a firm hold on what Jesus taught about manifesting abundance, and victories will begin to multiply.

To share your testimony, write to:

John Avanzini
c/o Partner Love Center
P.O. Box 917001
Ft. Worth, TX 76117-9001

Trinity Broadcasting Network

An all-Christian Television Network Broadcasting the
Gospel 24 hours a day via Satellite, Cable TV and
Local TV Broadcast Stations

Alphabetical Directory of TBN Owned and Affiliate Stations
(* Indicates an Affiliate-owned station)

ALASKA
•Anchorage Ch. 22
•Anchorage Ch.41
•North Pole Ch. 4
ALABAMA
•Berry Ch. 63
•Birmingham Ch. 51
•Decatur Ch. 22
•Dothan Ch. 41
•Florence Ch. 57
•Gadsden Ch. 60
•Huntsville Ch. 67
•Mobile Ch. 21
•Montgomery Ch. 45
•Opelika Ch. 35
Scottsboro Ch. 64
•Selma Ch. 52
•Tuscaloosa Ch. 46
ARKANSAS
•DeQueen Ch. 8
Fayetteville Ch. 42
Ft Smith Ch. 27
•Harrison Ch. 23
•Little Rock Ch. 33
Mountain Home Ch. 43
ARIZONA
Bullhead Ch. 20
Cottonwood Ch. 58
•Duncan Ch. 17
Flagstaff Ch. 62
Globe Ch. 63
•Lake Havasu Ch. 25
Phoenix Ch. 21
Shonto/Tonalea Ch. 38
•Sierra Vista Ch. 33
Tucson Ch. 57
Tucson Ch. 56
CALIFORNIA
Alturas Ch. 30
Atwater/Merced Ch. 57
Bakersfield Ch. 55
Chico Ch. 67
Coalinga Ch. 42
Desert Hot Springs Ch. 60
•Fresno Ch. 56
•Fresno Ch. 53

•Inyokern/Ridgecrest Ch. 53
Lancaster/Palmdale Ch. 54
•Lompoc Ch. 23
Mariposa Ch. 28
Monterey Ch. 53
•Morro Bay Ch. 22
Palm Springs Ch. 66
Porterville/Visalia Ch. 15
Redding Ch. 65
Sacramento Ch. 69
• Salinas/Santa Cruz Ch. 33
• San Jose/Santa Clara Ch. 22
•San Luis Obispo Ch. 36
Santa Ana Ch. 40
Santa Barbara Ch. 15
•Santa Maria Ch. 65
Ventura Ch. 45
Victorville Ch. 33
COLORADO
•Boulder Ch. 17
•Colorado Springs, Ch. 43
Denver Ch. 57
Denver Ch. 66
Denver Ch. 33
•LaJunta Ch. 35
•Lamar Ch. 42
•Las Animas Ch. 40
Loveland Ch. 48
•Pueblo Ch 48
DELAWARE
Dover Ch. 67
•Wilmington Ch. 40
FLORIDA
•Alachua Ch. 69
Fort Meyers Ch. 67
•Fort Pierce Ch. 21
•Jacksonville Ch. 59
Lake City Ch. 23
•Leesburg/Orlando Ch. 55
•Melbourne Ch. 62
Miami Ch. 45
Sebring Ch. 17
St Petersburg Ch. 60
•Tallahassee Ch. 17
Tampa Ch. 68
West Palm Beach Ch. 47

GEORGIA
Albany Ch. 23
Augusta Ch. 65
Brunswick Ch. 33
•Dalton Ch. 23
•Hazelhurst Ch. 63
Marietta Ch. 55
Monroe/Atlanta Ch. 63
Savannah Ch. 67
•Thomasville Ch. 22
Tifton Ch. 20
Valdosta Ch. 66
Waycross Ch. 46
HAWAII
•Wailuku Ch. 61
IOWA
•Ames Ch. 52
Cedar Rapids Ch. 61
Davenport/
    Cedar Rapids Ch. 58
•Des Moines Ch. 35
•Iowa City Ch. 64
•Keokuk Ch. 60
Ottumwa Ch. 42
•Sioux City Ch. 38
Waterloo Ch. 65
IDAHO
Boise Ch. 47
Coeur d' Alene Ch. 53
Pocatello Ch. 15
ILLINOIS
•Bloomington Ch. 64
Champaign/Urbana Ch. 34
Decatur Ch. 29
•La Salle Ch. 35
•Marion Ch. 27
Palatine Ch. 36
•Peoria Ch. 41
•Quincy Ch. 16
•Robinson Ch. 57
Rockford Ch. 52
•Sterling Ch. 52
Waukegan Ch. 22
INDIANA
•Angola/Ft Wayne Ch. 63
Bloomington Ch. 42

•Clarksville Ch. 26
Elkhart Ch. 67
Evansville Ch. 38
•Fort Wayne Ch. 66
•Jeffersonville Ch. 05
Lafayette Ch. 36
•Muncie Ch. 32
Richmond Ch. 43
Terre Haute Ch. 65
KANSAS
Junction City Ch. 25
Manhattan Ch. 31
Salina Ch. 15
Topeka Ch. 21
Wichita Ch. 59
KENTUCKY
•Beattyville Ch. 65
Corbin Ch 41
• East Bernstadt Ch. 09
Hopkinsville Ch. 62
•Paducah Ch. 54
LOUISANA
Alexandria Ch. 19
Baton Rouge Ch. 56
•Lake Charles Ch. 51
Mermentau Ch. 45
Monroe Ch. 27
New Iberia Ch. 49
New Orleans Ch. 59
Shreveport Ch. 65
MAINE
Bangor Ch. 17
Danforth Ch. 17
Dover/Foxcroft Ch.19
Farmington Ch. 21
Machias Ch. 21
Madawaska Ch. 17
Medway Ch. 14
•Portland Ch. 18
Presque Isle Ch.51
MARYLAND
Cresaptown/
  Cumberland Ch. 16
MICHIGAN
Detroit Ch. 66
•Iron Mountain Ch. 08
•Jackson Ch. 59
•Kalamazoo Ch. 24
•Lansing Ch. 69
Muskegon Ch. 29
•Muskegon Ch. 54
•Saginaw Ch. 49
MINNESOTA
Duluth Ch. 58
•Fairmont Ch. 28

Minneapolis Ch. 58
Rochester Ch. 60
St Cloud Ch. 19
•Wilmar Ch. 27
MISSISSIPPI
Biloxi Ch. 29
•Bruce Ch. 7
•Calhoun City Ch. 34
Columbus Ch. 25
Grenada Ch. 25
•Jackson Ch. 64
MISSOURI
•Anderson /
  Pineville Ch. 09
•Branson Ch. 25
Columbia Ch. 56
•Jeffersonson City Ch. 41
•Joplin/Carthage Ch. 46
•Monett Ch. 38
•Neosho Ch. 32
Poplar Bluff Ch.39
Springfield Ch. 52
St Charles Ch. 34
•St Joseph Ch. 16
•St Louis Ch. 18
MONTANA
•Billings Ch. 14
•Bozeman Ch. 45
Great Falls Ch. 53
Helena Ch. 41
Kalispell Ch. 26
NEBRASKA
•Council Bluffs/
  Omaha Ch. 45
Lincoln Ch. 39
Ogallala Ch. 26
NEVADA
Carson City Ch. 19
Las Vegas Ch. 57
Reno Ch. 45
NEW JERSEY
Atlantic City Ch. 36
•Cape May/
  Wildwood Ch. 05
NEW MEXICO
•Alamogordo Ch. 29
•Albuquerque Ch. 23
•Carlsbad Ch. 63
•Clovis Ch. 65
•Elida Ch. 36
•Farmington Ch. 47
•Hobbs Ch. 18
Raton Ch. 18
•Roswell Ch. 27
•Roswell Ch. 44

•Roswell Ch. 33
•Ruidoso Ch. 47
NEW YORK
Albany Ch. 64
Binghampton Ch. 14
•Buffalo Ch. 49
Glens Falls Ch. 14
Jamestown Ch. 10
•Massena Ch. 20
Olean Ch. 22
Poughkeepsie Ch. 54
•Rochester Ch. 59
Utica Ch. 41
NORTH CAROLINA
•Asheville Ch. 69
Charlotte Ch. 68
•Gastonia Ch. 62
Goldsboro Ch. 59
Goldsboro Ch. 56
Greenville Ch. 54
•Hendersonville Ch. 31
Raleigh Ch. 38
Statesville Ch. 66
Wilmington Ch. 20
NORTH DAKOTA
Fargo Ch. 56
Grand Forks Ch. 22
•Rolette Ch. 20
Williston Ch. 40
OHIO
Canton Ch. 17
Chillicothe Ch. 40
•Columbus Ch. 24
Dayton Ch. 68
Kirtland/Cleveland Ch. 51
Lexington Ch. 32
• Marietta Ch. 26
•Marion Ch. 39
Portsmouth Ch. 21
•Sandusky Ch. 52
•Seaman Ch. 17
Springfield Ch. 47
•Toledo (North) Ch. 68
•Toledo (South) Ch 46
Youngstown Ch. 39
Zanesville Ch. 36
OKLAHOMA
Ardmore Ch. 44
•Balko Ch. 25
•Bartlesville Ch. 17
•Elk City Ch. 52
•Guymon Ch. 53
Lawton Ch. 27
Oklahoma City Ch. 14
•Sayre Ch. 26

•Strong City Ch. 30
OREGON
Bend Ch. 33
Coos Bay Ch. 33
•Cottage Grove Ch. 50
•Eugene Ch. 59
Grants Pass Ch. 59
Klamath Falls Ch. 58
Lakeview Ch. Ch. 21
Medford Ch. 57
•Portland Ch. 24
Roseburg Ch. 14
PENNSYLVANIA
Erie Ch. 42
•Kingston Ch. 54
Meadville Ch. 52
State College Ch. 42
Williamsport Ch. 39
SOUTH CAROLINA
Anderson Ch. 18
Charleston Ch. 44
•Columbia Ch.51
•Greenville Ch. 16
Myrtle Beach Ch. 66
•Myrtle Beach Ch. 43
Orangeburg Ch. 52
SOUTH DAKOTA
Aberdeen Ch. 20
Brookings Ch. 15
Huron Ch. 38
Madison Ch. 27
Rapid City Ch. 33
Sioux Falls Ch. 66
Yankton Ch. 31
TENNESSEE
Cookeville Ch. 46
Farragut Ch. 66
•Hendersonville Ch. 50
Jackson Ch. 35
•Memphis Ch. 65
•Memphis//Hly
   Springs MS Ch.40
Morristown Ch. 31
•Nashville Ch. 36
TEXAS
Abilene Ch. 51
•Amarillo Ch. 20
Austin Ch.63
•Beaumont Ch. 34
•Big Spring Ch. 30
Brownwood Ch.26
College Station Ch. 47
Corpus Christi Ch. 57
Dallas Ch. 58
•Ft. Stockton/Alpine Ch. 30

•Greenville Ch. 53
•Harlingen Ch. 44
•Houston Ch. 14
• Huntsville Ch. 31
•Kerrville Ch. 02
•Killeen Ch. 31
Kingsville Ch. 31
•La Mesa Ch. 47
•Livingston Ch. 66
•Longview Ch. 10
•Lufkin Ch. 05
•Monahans Ch. 28
•Odessa Ch. 42
Palestine Ch. 17
Paris Ch. 42
•Pecos Ch. 64
San Angelo Ch. 19
San Antonio Ch.33
San Antonio Ch. 20
•Snyder Ch. 26
•Texarkana Ch. 30
•Tyler Ch. 20
Victoria Ch. 43
•Wichita Falls Ch. 26
UTAH
Ogden Ch. 64
•Salt Lake City Ch.36
Vernal Ch. 39
VIRGINIA
•Danville Ch. 18
•Front Royal/Winchstr Ch.
28
•Harrisonburg Ch24
Lynchburg Ch. 32
Roanoke Ch. 49
•Winchester Ch. 48
•Woodstock Ch. 10
VERMONT
Burlington Ch. 16
WASHINGTON
Aberdeen Ch. 23
Ellensburg Ch. 39
•Longview Ch. 36
•Richland Ch. 49
Spokane Ch. 55
Tacoma/Seattle Ch. 20
•Wenatchee Ch. 13
•Wenatchee Ch. 59
•Yakima Ch. 64
WISCONSIN
Green Bay Ch.68
Janesville Ch. 19
•La Crosse Ch. 44
Madison Ch. 33
Ripon Ch. 42

Sheboygan Ch. 20
Waupaca Ch.55
WEST VIRGINIA
•Charleston Ch. 45
•Huntington Ch. 19
Parkersburg Ch. **39**
WYOMING
•Casper Ch. 13
Green River Ch. 35

**INTERNATIONAL
STATIONS**

CENTRAL AMERICA

BELIZE
Belize City Ch. 23
COSTA RICA
St. Jose Ch. 23
Santa Elena Ch. 53
Cerro De La Muerte Ch.
53
Limon Ch. 23
Zapotal Ch 53
EL SALVADOR
El Salvador Ch. 25
HONDURAS
Tegulcigalpa Ch. 57
NICARAGUA
Managua Ch. 21
Eslteli Ch. 25
LaGateda Ch. 27 (under
   const.)

SOUTH AMERICA
ARGENTINA
Buenas Aires Ch. 68
BOLIVIA
LaPas Ch. 27
BRAZIL
Manaus Ch. 8
Porto Velho Ch. 6
CHILE
Santiago Ch. 50 (under
   const.)
COLUMBIA
Cali
ECUADOR
Quito Ch. 27
Guayaquil Ch 28

AFRICA
BOPHUTHATSWANA
CISKEI, SA
•Bisho Ch. 24

LESOTHO, SA
•Maseru
NAMIBIA, SA
Windhoek
TRANSKEI, SA
•Umata Ch. 67
Butterworth Ch. 25
Mt. Ayliff Ch. 27
Ikwezi/Ngangelizwe Ch. 51
Queenstown Ch. 10
Port. St. Johns Ch. 65
Engcoro Ch. 49 (under
    const.)
Mount Fletcher Ch. 51
    (under const.)

**REPUBLIC OF
SOUTH AFRICA**
•TV 1 Channel 13
•TV 2 Channel 9
SWAZILAND
•Mbabane
ZAMBIA
Lukasa

**SOUTH PACIFIC
KINGDOM OF TONGA**
Nuku-Alofa A3M Ch. 7

**EUROPE
ALBANIA**
Various Government-
owned Channels

ICELAND
Reykjavik Ch. 53 and 45

**ITALY
Lombardia Region**
Agno Magnaso Ch. 39
Biella Ch. 59
Campione Ch. 44
Como, Ch. 28
Ivrea Ch. 36
Maccaagno Ch. 45
Milano Ch. 11
Pavia Certosa Ch. H1
Porto Ceresio Ch. 468
Valdosta Ch. 28
Varese Ch. 33
Viggiu Ch. 46
Piemonte Region
Torre Bert Ch. 60
Piazza Lancia Ch. 10
Pecetto Torino Ch. 27

LaMorra Ch. 60
Guarene Ch. 28
Azzano Ch. 29
St. Stafano Ch. 48
Mombaruzzo Ch. 68
Bricco Olio Ch. H2
Monte Ronzone Ch. 29
Corio Ch. 60
Nieve Ch. 42
Canale Ch. 26
Dogliani Ch. 21
Somano Ch. 42
Paroldo Ch. 42
St. Michele Mondovi Ch. 68
Alba Bricco Capre Ch. 68
Lazio Region
Rome Ch. 33
Rome/Mt. Cavo Ch. 47
P. Nibbio Ch. 64
Mt.. Calcarone Ch. 50
Mt. Artemisio Ch. 35
Rocca d'Arce Ch. 47
Fumone Ch. 39
Arpino Ch. 48
Valle Maio Ch. 61
Rocca Monfina Ch. 50
Mt. Orlando Ch. 48
Avezzano Ch. 31
Mt. Cicoli Ch. 42
Segni Ch. 34
Vicalvi Ch. 63
Montattico Ch. 53
Capistrello Ch. 29
Civita d'Antino Ch. 673
Meta Ch. 58
Isola Liri Ch. 24
Subiaco Ch. 22
Gadamello Ch. 26
Mt. Amita, Ch. 47
Mt. Paradiso Ch. 61
Scansano Ch. 54
Mt. St. Biagio Ch. 57
St. di Fondi Ch. 24
St. Felice Circeo, Ch. 43
Secca Volsci Ch. 49
St. Vito Romano Ch. 44
Castro Volsci Ch. 31
St. Incarico Ch. 41
Itri Ch. 24
Balsorano Ch. 35
Pesche Ch. 58

GREECE
Athens Ch. 62

Corinth Ch. 54
Macedonia Ch. 62

SWITZERLAND
Locarno Ch. 37

RUSSIA
St. Petersburg Ch. 40
Moscow Ch. 3

**CARIBBEAN
GRAND CAYMAN**
Grand Cayman Ch. 21

GRENADA
St. George's Ch. 13

HAITI
Port-Au-Prince Ch. 16

NEVIS
Charlestown Ch. 13

ST. LUCIA
Castries Ch. 13

**TBN
SHORTWAVE RADIO**

**KTBN SUPERPOWER
SHORTWAVE RADIO**
St. Lake City, Utah
    8 AM - 4 PM (PST)
    15.590 MHGz.
    4 PM - 8 AM (PST)
    7.510 MHz
    *(Reaching Around
    the World)*

RADIO PARADISE
ST. KITTS, W.I.
830 KHz AM Radio
24 Hours a Day

**For More Information,
please write:**
TBN
P.O. Box A
Santa Ana, CA 92711
24-Hour Prayer Line
(714) 731-1000

GOD WANTS YOU TO BE DEBT FREE!

Now... through the Debt Free Army you can put His plan for your Debt-Free life-style into action.

As a member of the Debt Free Army, I will be able to personally guide you, step by step month by month, from the slavery of debt into the glorious experience of debt-free living. No matter what financial condition you're in, this strategically prepared material can take you steadily and rapidly out of debt. It's worked for others-it will work for you.

–John Avanzini

CALL TOLL FREE
1-800-FREE ARMY

To receive your FREE copy of HOW TO SAVE BIG MONEY ON YOUR UTILITY BILLS

Now you can have your own personal copy of this valuable 8-page, full-color supplement taken directly from the Debt Free Army's Battle Plan arsenal. Included in this money-saving piece are **40 ways** you can save from **$30 to $80 each month** on your utility bills -- And it will be sent to you absolutely FREE and postage paid when you **call 1- 800 - FREE ARMY**